CDT Design and Realization

COURSEWORK AND REVISION COMPANION

Trevor Bridges

GCSE

Charles Letts & Co Ltd
London, Edinburgh & New York

First published 1990
by Charles Letts & Co Ltd
Diary House, Borough Road, London SE1 1DW

Text: © Trevor Bridges 1990
Illustrations: Kevin Jones Associates
© Charles Letts & Co Ltd
Cover photograph: Steven Hunt, Image Bank
Handwriting samples: Artistic License

Students' work from a variety of sources , in particular:
Latymer School, Edmonton
William Ellis School, Parliament Hill
The English School's Foundation, Hong Kong
Some photography: Martin Black
Examination examplar material: London East Anglian Group

British Library Cataloguing in Publication Data
Bridges, Trevor
   CDT: Design and realization coursework and
   revision companion.
   1. England. Secondary schools. Curriculum subjects;
   Crafts, design & technology
   I. Title
   607.121242

   ISBN 0-85097-885-8

Printed and bound in Great Britain by
Charles Letts (Scotland) Ltd

Contents

Preface

This book would not have been possible but for the hard work of many students, the work of whom is illustrated in the following pages.
To them this book is dedicated. I am also indebted to the continued encouragement and help of Mike Rose who has assisted in the preparation of this book. I would also like to thank Bob Dunlop for reading the manuscript and generally being around when needed and also my wife and family who had to accept that I wasn't around often when I was needed. I am equally grateful to Larry Sampson and Tricia Andrews of the London East Anglian Group for providing help and exemplar material and to the subject officers of the following examination groups for their permission to reproduce examination questions:

London East Anglian Group
Midland Examining Group
Northern Examining Association
Southern Examining Group
Welsh Joint Education Committee

Introduction to coursework

What this book is about

This book will help you do well in your GCSE CDT:Design and Realization examinations. It doesn't matter which examination group sets the examination for which you are entered – the principles will be the same. You will probably have obtained this book somewhere part way through your school career and you are likely, already, to have had some CDT experience. Most schools tackle CDT in a similar way with your learning through 'doing'. This book will guide you through the different things which examiners will expect you to have experienced and done throughout your course. Most of your learning will be through 'design and make' projects and so this book concentrates on the 'design and make' process. The chart below should remind you of what this means.

It will not always be like this. Sometimes, for example, you may start by evaluating and decide to improve an existing product

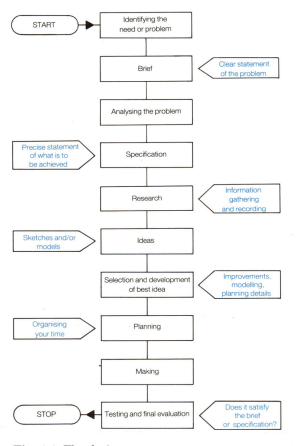

Fig. 1.1 The design process

During the two years of your GCSE course you will probably undertake two or three different projects which should be selected to allow you to gain as wide a range of experience as possible. In this book there are illustrations of actual candidates' work. These will give you a good idea what examiners are expecting and the quality of work which you should try to achieve in order to get a high grade. In addition the range of work and the techniques used should give you some ideas for your own projects.

Throughout this book you have the opportunity to assess the work of others and this will help you to assess your own work. Section Eight gives you the chance to test yourself on parts of the design process.

Section Nine is a guide to revision. The topics which examiners ask questions about are listed and there are clues about how examination questions will be assessed. You will of course be expected to know and understand more than just the bare outline given in this book but your teacher will have made sure that you have had a wide experience throughout your course. Some topics can be difficult to cover whilst working on your projects and so these are explained in a little more detail. Section Nine also includes some examination questions with an explanation of how they would be marked by an examiner, and gives you an opportunity to pretend you are the examiner and estimate what certain answers are worth. Understanding what the examiner is looking for will help you give the best answers. Finally, Section Nine has a number of examination questions with detailed sample answers given at the end. However, do remember that there are often a wide range of answers possible, although the answers that have been given would be likely to score very high marks.

Specifically design exams are not covered by this book but in many cases they are really only an extension of coursework: LEAG and MEG, for example, set a 'design and make' exam, much of which is assessed by the teacher just like coursework.

The importance of coursework

> *A lot of marks are awarded for coursework. Make sure you do it well*

A glance through any CDT syllabus will show you the importance placed on coursework. Anything from 30 to 50 per cent of the total marks can be gained from coursework. Those examination groups who allow only 30 to 40 per cent of the total marks also have a 'design and make' examination and adding the marks for that gives a total of 70 per cent of your marks. All these marks are gained without a formal examination.

A more important reason for coursework is that you learn most of your CDT knowledge and gain most of your understanding whilst working on your projects. Unlike many school subjects, practical work is not additional to 'theory' lessons. It is the main way you learn. By **designing** and **making** you will learn and understand and be able to apply both to new situations. You will then do well in design and written examinations.

Some people find that they do badly in formal examinations because they are nervous or they find it difficult to work under pressure. Others can have a bad day due to illness. Coursework, therefore, shows the examiners what you can really do.

Often coursework is thought of as only embracing 'total' 'design and make' projects, consisting of the complete design process from identifying a need to the finished article or system. However, it can consist of shorter, part processes. For example, you may be asked to develop a project only as far as the modelling stage, or evaluate a product manufactured by someone else.

Much coursework submitted for CDT:Design and Realization contains straightforward constructional work with little or no 'technology', but remember technological projects are encouraged by the examination groups. You are also encouraged to incorporate computer-aided design and information technology into your projects.

The regional examination groups have different requirements for the scope and content of coursework. These requirements are summarized overleaf. All six regional examinations groups are shown, but you will only be interested in the one for which you are to be entered.

Coursework requirements of the different examination groups	Examination group	Requirements for assessment	Marks as a percentage of the total for the whole exam	
	LEAG	A selection of the best work produced during the last two years of the course, including one complete design folder. Although not displayed all coursework must be available	40	70
		The realization from your 'design and make' examination	15	
		The design part is sent away for marking	15	
	MEG	All work must be available for assessment, but 'credit' will be given for the best work you have done	30	70
		Your 'design and make' project including the design folder	40	
	NEA	A 'design and make' project undertaken during the 12 months prior to the exam. Several small projects are allowed but all project folders must be submitted	50	
	SEG	One major project or two or three smaller ones. These must show a wide range of knowledge and skill. Each project must be accompanied by a design folder. The 'making' part of coursework carries more marks than the folder part. Credit will be given to the best work	50	
	WJEC	A design study chosen from a selection of five. You may however select a topic of your own choosing. It should represent 12 months' work	50	
	NISEC	All coursework including one project chosen from a selection of six design briefs provided by the examination group	50	

How will you earn your marks for coursework?

Introduction

At the beginning of this book you were reminded that coursework consists mostly of projects which take you through the process of design. Designing begins with recognizing a problem, need or opportunity and finishes when the problem has been solved, need has been fully satisfied or the opportunity exploited. In between there are a number of stages and throughout it is often necessary to go back to an earlier stage to check that you are doing what you intended. Examiners expect you to have worked through this process and will reward the work you have done at all stages.

'Don't do your design work after you have made your project!'

Some candidates think that all they have to do is make something and afterwards produce some pretty drawings and everything will be alright. Nothing could be further from the truth. The making part of a project will not normally gain more than one half of the marks and producing a few drawings *after* the making is completed will gain hardly any extra at all!

Examiners will assess what you do and so it is important to keep everything and organize it in a folder or folio (more of this in Section Six). Examiners want to see evidence that you have organized yourself and used your time well. They realize that there are many pressures on you with other GCSE subjects requiring projects but this is all the more reason for organizing your time. You need to be critical about your own work and unwarranted self-congratulation is certainly not what is wanted. Throughout a project you will need to make decisions about it and you should record those decisions and the reasons for them. Finally, you will need to make an evaluation of the finished project, give recommendations for improvements and comment on the way you went about completing it.

All these aspects of your coursework will be assessed by the examiners and each examination group allocates marks for each part. The marks awarded for Making Skills are similar to the mark awarded for Design and Evaluation Skills.

The following sections, indicated by the symbol explain the parts of your work which the examiners will assess. Alongside each is a box indicating the maximum marks awarded for this topic by at least one examination group. Broadly speaking similar marks are awarded by each of the examination groups.

Identifying a need, the design brief, analysis, research and writing a specification

Up to **5** per cent of your marks

Identifying a need

There are two types of need, real and imaginary.
Seeing papers scattered all over a desk and constantly falling on the floor suggests that there is a need to organize them by means of a rack, tray, paperweight or something similar, or perhaps to throw them away! This is a **real** need.

Guessing that a braille map needs to be provided at the entrance to your school for the use of blind visitors is probably an **imaginary** need. How many blind visitors does your school get? Do they have many difficulties finding their way around? Providing a braille map may be a useful thing to do but you can't describe it as a need unless you have reason to think that it is necessary. If a manufacturing company, for example, produced something based on simply guessing what it thought was needed it would probably have difficulty selling it.

Needs can arise from the following situations:

Try to make your project satisfy a real need

- Changed circumstances, e.g. going to a new school.

- Previous solutions no longer satisfying the need, e.g. record players being too bulky to carry around.

- Observing someone having difficulties, e.g. a parent trying to 'navigate' a supermarket trolley, two children and a pushchair to a car.

- Being asked to provide a solution to a need specified by others, e.g. an examination question or a brief set by the teacher.

Needs are all around you and when looking for one it will be easiest to search in areas which are familiar to you. You can look at home, at school, observe friends, and consider your amusement and entertainment activities.

For example, one student recognized that litter was not only untidy but also a waste of natural resources. He decided on a project to convert waste paper into briquettes suitable for burning in a solid fuel stove. He expressed the need in his design folio in this way:

Fig. 2.1 A student identified a need

Do you think it clearly expresses the problem?
What other projects does it suggest to you?

You will read more about identifying needs in Section Five.

Expressing a brief in a design folio

A well-expressed brief can be simple, to the point and should be expressed neatly. It should explain what the problem is and say what you intend to do about it.

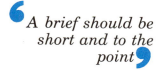
A brief should be short and to the point

> Design Brief
>
> An elderly lady is having difficulty turning on the bath taps because she has lost the strength in her hands. Devise a method which will enable her to turn on and off the bath taps.

Fig. 2.2 A well-expressed brief

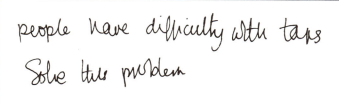

people have difficulty with taps
Solve this problem

Fig. 2.3 A badly expressed design brief

In this example the candidate has really not said what is being attempted. The presentation is poor. It would be difficult for someone else to develop this project further with any certainty of what the real problem was. If **your** handwriting is this difficult to read then you should consider typing your brief.

Hints for writing design briefs

1 *Make it short and to the point*
2 *Include only relevant details*
3 *Don't give a hint of a solution*
4 *Use broad terms such as 'container' or 'system' rather than specific terms such as 'box' or 'filing cabinet'*
5 *Highlight **key** words, i.e. elderly, bath, strength, hands*

Analysing the problem

Analysing a problem means dividing it into key parts, asking questions **and** providing answers. You can begin by making a list of all the things you want to find out about and listing where you might go for answers. You should go to the place which most easily gives you the answer to your question.

	Question	Where to go for answer
1	Does the old lady have the same problem with both taps?	Telephone or visit lady
2	What are the dimensions of the taps?	Go to lady's home
3	How much room is there next to the bath?	Go to lady's home

cont'd

| 4 Would differently shaped taps help? | Go to plumber's merchant and lady's home |
| 5 Can the plumbing be modified? (AND SO ON) | Discuss with a plumber |

Fig. 2.4 List the questions to which you need answers

There is more advice about analysing and thinking about problems in Section Five.

When you have analysed your problem, you will need to do research in order to collect information to help you to design a solution. This research must be presented in your design folder.

Drawing up a specification

A specification is a set of targets which you will try to achieve. It will outline the restrictions placed upon you by the problem. It needs to be as open as possible and allow as wide a range of solutions as possible but it must contain considerably more detail than the brief. It must also contain those factors over which you have no control, such as maximum size allowed or time deadlines.

'A specification is a set of targets which you will try to achieve'

Suppose you have been asked to design a 'first aid kit for a hiker'. Your specification might be something like this:

```
The first aid kit must:

1 Contain all the necessary medical kit.(list the contents)

2 Be small enough to be carried in the outside pocket of a
  day rucksack.

3 Be waterproof.

4 Have no sharp edges or corners.

5 Have separate compartments for the corners.

6 Be able to be made with the school facilities.

7 Be able to be made by me.

8 Be able to be made in the time available.(state how long
  it might take in hours)

9 Be able to be tested so that an evaluation can be made at
  the end.
```

Fig. 2.5 Example of a specification

Note: points 6, 7, 8 and 9 are common to all projects but you should include them anyway for completeness. You would however get most of your marks for those points which are particular to the problem.

A candidate drew up the next specification for a solution to the 'bath tap problem' (see earlier). The notes at the side suggest errors which have been made.

*What do **you** think of it?*

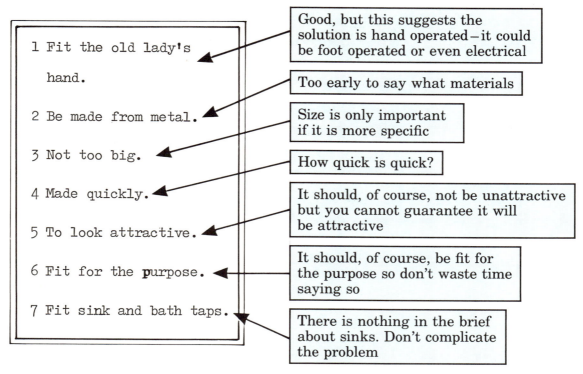

Fig. 2.6 A specification

Although this is well presented it is badly expressed and will not help to produce a good solution. It is unrealistic and far too limiting. It does not allow for a wide range of solutions.

Here is another specification presented in a different way.

> *What details would **you** add?*

When cooking, people often boil more than one thing at once, and may also do other things at the same time as the cooking, and so will leave the things which are boiling unattended, and won't watch them.

My project is therefore to make a device which will sound a warning and/or cut off the heat supply when the liquid which is being heated begins to boil over.

This device will mean that the person who is doing the cooking is able to do other work while the food or liquid is cooking without worrying about it, and will not have to keep returning to the cooker to check the things which are boiling.

SPECIFICATION

1 Have a warning which is loud enough to be heard throughout the house.

2 Be as small, light, and compact as possible.

3 Be resistant to both heat and water.

4 Be cheap to construct and buy if it were on sale in shops.

5 Be clean and cleanable as it will be used close to food items.

6 Be strong as it may be in a position where a lot of activity is taking place, and so it could be hit in some way.

7 Be electrically safe.

cont'd

cont'd

Other things which should be considered when making the device are:—

1 What type of equipment it will be used on. Possible items of of equipment which the device may have to be fixed onto are:—

(a) Saucepans of various sizes.

(b) Cup/Mugs.

(c) Kettle/Coffee Pot.

(d) Dishes of various sizes.

2 Another consideration is whether the device will be used in a microwave oven or not.

Fig. 2.7 A student's specification

Hints for your analysis

1 *Break down the problem into key parts*
2 *Ask questions which will need researching*
3 *Get answers from the most appropriate source*
4 *Record your findings in your folio*

Hints for drawing up specifications

1 *A specification is a set of targets*
2 *You will need a specification so that you can test and evaluate*
3 *Make your targets realistic*
4 *Don't make your targets contradict each other*
5 *Make your targets specific if necessary, e.g. minimum and maximum sizes*
6 *Don't try to achieve more than is asked for in the brief*

Research

The purpose of doing research is to help you do your project better. Since you will be solving a problem or satisfying a need research will be necessary to make this possible and to enable you to produce the best possible result. Research is **not** undertaken in order to pad out your folio or to impress the examiner that you have done lots of work. Therefore, the golden rule is: **if you don't need the information to help solve the problem, then don't waste time doing it!**

Searching for information can be a difficult task so do try to avoid wasting too much time. You can either get information from someone else, by reading a book, asking someone questions, or cutting out sections from newspapers and magazines. Because you will be using and examining the work of someone else this is called **secondary research**.

You can also undertake a survey or do experiments yourself and this will allow you to find out things which cannot be obtained from secondary research. Because you do the research yourself, this is called **primary research**.

You may need to find out information by **experiment**. You could, for example, find out what 'finish' will look best by applying a variety of finishes and then asking other people's opinions. You might also want to find out what shapes children like or what colour is best for a kitchen appliance. You should record your findings and where appropriate take photographs.

Primary research can take a long time and so before spending time on it first check that the information you need is not available from secondary sources.

What kind of information do you need?

Sometimes it can be very frustrating to have to wait for a reply from a letter. Do you now telephone or would it have been better to have telephoned in the first place? Do you really know what you want to find out anyway? Simply asking for 'some information about materials' won't be much good either.

The kind of information which you will need is likely to be one or more of the following:

- Background information.
- Evidence to back up a theory or idea.
- Gaps in the market.
- Ideas.
- Guidance with an idea.
- Technical information.
- Other sources of information.

A chart in Appendix 4 of this book shows you some of the places you can go to for information. Use it carefully and it could save you a lot of potentially wasted time. Begin by deciding what kind of information you need.

Make sure that in some way or other the following information is included in your project folder:

- What you did.
- Where you went.
- Who you spoke to.
- What questions you asked.
- What you found out.
- The importance of the information you obtained.

> *Imagine you need information about litter bins. Where would* **you** *go for help? List those places, beginning with the most obvious*

Hints for good research

1 *Know exactly what you want to find out*
2 *Go to the source of information which is most convenient*
3 *Record all your findings carefully*
4 *Choose an effective way to present them*

Generating ideas

Getting ideas is the most difficult part of your project

Getting ideas can be the most difficult part of any project. Once you have ideas it is easier to see how they can be improved. When trying to generate ideas it might be useful to consider the following points:

- Most designing is for people.
- People will be much happier if they can use things safely and in comfort.
- Well-designed things work properly.
- Designs need to be pleasant to look at and live with.

> Up to
> **5** per cent of your marks

Comfort

Seats must be the right shape and size to be comfortable. If you have ever sat cramped in the back of a small car you will know what it can be like to not have enough leg room. You will also realize how uncomfortable it can be to work at a table which is too high or too low in relation to the chair you are sitting on.

Safety

Whenever you can you must make sure that your designs are safe. If you are making toys, for example, you must avoid sharp edges and painting with lead-based (poisonous) paints. Remember, the elderly and the young are particularly at risk.

Ergonomics

This is making sure objects, systems and environments are designed so that people can use them easily with the minimum of effort. Care is taken to design the dashboard of a car so that everything is easy to reach and the steering wheel is at the most suitable angle.

Anthropometrics

This is a science and is concerned with measuring the dimensions and limits of the human body. A chart on page 158 of this book will give you some of the more important anthropometric information. In the design of a car anthropometric information is used to ensure that seats fit and support the human body. They are often adjustable so that they can be made to fit different sized people.

Function

Put simply, the function of an object is what it does. You will have to think carefully of doing things different ways. Consider the 'bath tap problem'. You could, of course, design an attachment for the tap which would be easier to grip or hold. But it might be easier for the old lady if you were able to connect the attachment to levers and make it capable of operation by the foot. A solenoid valve (like the ones inside automatic washing machines) could be fitted.

Appearance

Appearance is the way things look. Everything has appearance but not everything is pleasing and what is pleasing to one person may seem unattractive to another. It will help if you consider the following:
- Careful use of good proportions (see Section Nine).
- Simple shapes without too many 'decorative' bits.
- Colours and patterns which fit in with the proposed surroundings, and appropriate textures will all help to make your solution better.

Getting good ideas

- You can't expect to be immediately inspired so ask questions. For example, what are the main points of the problem? Are there other products which do a similar thing? You might be designing something to keep the top of your desk or dressing table tidy. Think about other products which are used for keeping things tidy: book racks, washing lines, dustbins, shelves, a car glove compartment, and a computer workstation.
- Make comparisons. Saying what the strengths and weaknesses of other things are may help you to come up with new suggestions.
- Brainstorming. Either working alone or as a group can produce a whole range of ideas. You can read more about this in Section Five.

Brilliant ideas!

Your first idea is seldom the most appropriate

You may think that the first idea you have is all that you need. You may think that it satisfies all of the specification. It's very easy to go ahead and start making your idea. Experience has shown that there are very few inspirational ideas which are not capable of improvement. Even if you are blessed with a talent to solve all parts of a problem with a blinding flash of inspiration, how will you ever know that it is the best idea you are capable of unless you consider others? However much you think your first idea is perfect you must resist the temptation to rush on to making it. You **should** consider other ideas or at the very least take care to **develop** your first idea. If you don't you may be disappointed with the final result and you will almost certainly **not** get the highest marks!

- Try to show ideas which indicate different ways of solving the problem (as shown in the 'bath tap problem').

- Showing ideas which are a simple variation on a theme (six different shapes for bath tap handle extensions) is likely to score you less marks.

- Draw accurately in two and three dimensions and add colour or shading to make your ideas appear clearer.

- Be careful to add notes to your ideas indicating the good and weak points. It is a good idea to keep checking back to your specification. It is not important to make your early (initial) ideas fantastic works of art, rough drawings will do.

- Add details of materials, methods of construction, sizes, and so on.

Candidates who show their ideas with clear accurate drawings and add explanatory notes (but not long essays) will get the highest marks. It is important to name materials and make sure you are specific. Simply writing 'wood' is not very helpful. 'Hardwood' is better but you should try to give more detail, e.g. 'Beech'. Do however check that you will be able to get hold of the material you choose. As an example, have a look at these ideas one candidate had for a 'fuse tester'.

> *Do you think he will get a lot of credit for them?*

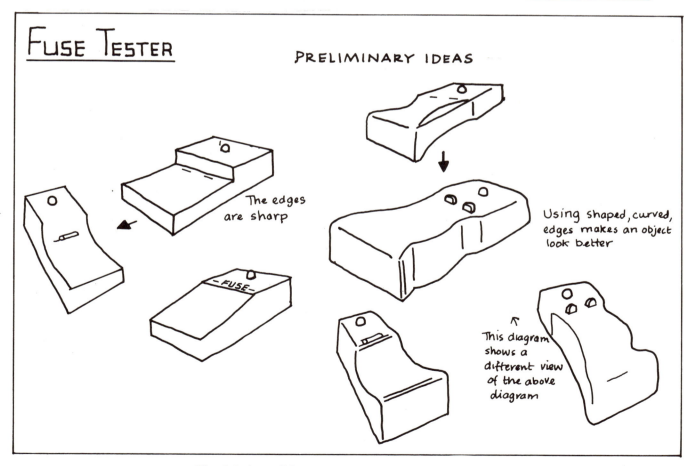

Fig. 2.8 A candidate's ideas

All these ideas are really only variations on a theme. They are clearly drawn but little information is given about materials, function or construction.

In the next example the candidate shows a range of ideas. They are not particularly well drawn but they do show a wide range of thinking about the problem which was to design a learning toy for a young child.

> *Can you think of ways to improve the communication of these ideas? Try consulting Section Three for ideas*

Fig. 2.9 A variety of ideas

Selecting suitable materials and manufacturing processes

Having ideas of what designs may look like may not be too difficult. Choosing suitable materials and deciding how they should be worked is more difficult. The following chart may help you decide on suitable materials and manufacturing processes.

'*Remember that different materials have different properties*'

Desired shape	Possible materials	Manufacturing processes
Straight lines, corners at right angles	Timber, acrylic	Glued joints
Smooth curves in one direction only	Aluminium sheet steel, acrylic	Bend around former
Hollow and lightweight	Rigid polystyrene	Vacuum formed or plug and yoke

cont'd

cont'd

Desired shape	Possible materials	Manufacturing processes
Circular hollow shapes	Rigid polystyrene, acrylic, copper, aluminium	Blow moulding. Beaten to shape with mallet
Circular solid shapes	Timber, mild steel, acrylic	Turned on lathe
Tubular shapes	Mild steel: square or round	Often welded together
Awkward strong shapes	Aluminium	Cast in sand mould
Strong curved shapes	Mild steel	Beaten to shape hot, on an anvil

Fig. 2.10 Selecting a suitable material and process

The important point to note here is that the shape and function of a component will determine the properties of the materials from which it is made.

Selecting and developing the best idea and producing a working drawing

Up to **10** per cent of your marks

You are sure to think that all or most of your ideas are good ones, after all if they are not good ideas why did you bother to draw them? The problem you now have is deciding which idea you are going to select

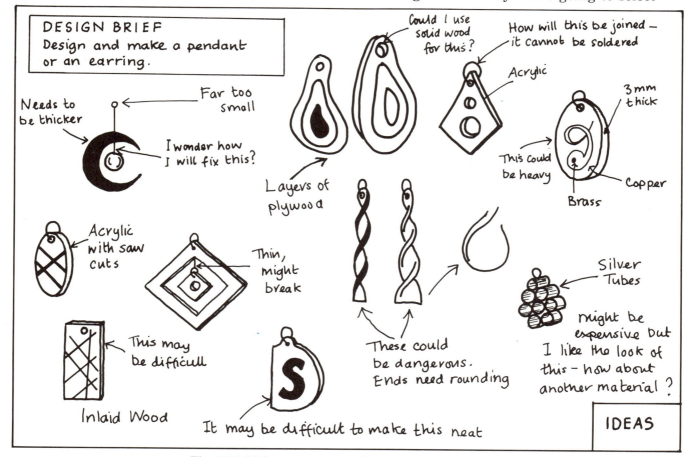

Fig. 2.11 Make notes on your drawings

and develop further. You will need to consider a whole range of things and so the result will have to be a compromise. Look through your ideas and try to identify positive and weak points. Add brief notes to your ideas like the ones in the example shown in Fig. 2.11. If it can be assumed that none of your ideas can be ruled out completely (e.g. not able to be made in the time, or too large, etc) then drawing a chart like the one shown in Fig. 2.13 may help.

Estimating the cost of an idea

Do try to remember that cost, for example, is not simply the cost of the materials. You should try to take into account labour, heating and lighting, wear and tear on equipment and electricity to run machines. You will need to find out the cost of materials and components from catalogues. Appendix 3 gives a useful listing of the costs of commonly-used materials. In making decisions about costings it is possible to use computer software. A computer program for the BBC computer is produced by the Banking Information Service and your school is likely to have a copy.

If you use this program you will need to check that the costings are up to date

```
ACRYLIC SHEET PPX      0.38          .2        0.08
LED RED                0.06          1         0.06
1.5V BATT AA ALK       0.28          1         0.28
CARDBOARD 300X100      0.02          2         0.04
R POLYSTYRENE 1MM      0.12          4         0.48
BATT HOLDER      AA    0.10          1         0.10
GLASSPAPER P.SHEET     0.07          .3        0.02
SOLDER                 0.10          0.25      0.03
INS WIRE               0.01          1         0.01

Total:       1.09
```

This is above my budget. The most expensive item is polystyrene sheet (48p – Vac forming). I can combine the use with another student and reduce the cost to 24p, this will make the total cost 85p which is within my budget.

Fig. 2.12 A print out from the BIS program

You are now in a position to make a selection from your ideas.

- Begin by making a list of what you consider the most important points and writing them on the left hand side of the chart (shown in Fig. 2.13).

- Estimate how well each solution satisfies each point by giving a mark out of five for each point: nothing out of five = hopeless, five out of five = excellent!

- Enter the marks on the chart.

- From the totals choose the one with the highest overall mark as the best possible solution.

If two have almost the same score then you might like to consider which point is the most important. For example, could it be cost? Or could it be ease of manufacture?

> *Could **you** decide which is more important?*

	IDEA 1	IDEA 2	IDEA 3
EASE OF USE	1	3	5
COST	3	1	2
SIZE	4	5	2
EASE OF MAKING	3	3	3
RELIABILITY	2	4	3
SURVEY OF POSSIBLE USES	1	3	2
BEST AT SOLVING PROBLEMS	1	2	3
TOTAL	15	21	20

Best idea

Fig. 2.13 Selecting your best idea

It may be necessary to ask for other people's opinions in order to make some decisions and you will need to do research and perhaps a survey of your friends or those who are likely to use the product you are designing.

Hints for generating ideas

1 *Look for ideas from a range of sources*
2 *Show a range of ideas which are not just variations on a theme*
3 *Express your ideas clearly by drawing and **brief** notes*
4 *Select the best idea as a compromise*

Developing your chosen idea (synthesis)

This is an opportunity to perfect and improve your chosen idea. You may, for example, have selected an idea which basically is a commercial solution to a similar problem or need. You now have the opportunity to alter it so that it fits exactly the specification for **your** solution. Initially your ideas will have little technical detail. During this next stage you must also be expected to consider details. These details can include:

- Function: will it work and be ergonomic?
- Selection of materials: will they do the job?
- Costing: are there cheaper ways of doing it just as well?
- Construction: how is it put together?
- Technical details: are they accurately shown?
- Aesthetics: does it look right for its task, for its surroundings, for me?
- Dimensions: are the sizes suitable for the task, available materials and standard forms? And are they accurately shown?
- Safety: will it be safe for the user and others?

Hints for developing ideas

1 *Make changes which you believe will be improvements*
2 *Do not change too much at once*
3 *Check that materials/facilities will be available*
4 *Can **you** make what you are proposing in the time available?*

Working drawings (or production drawing)

It is not necessary to always produce a three-view working drawing, indeed sometimes only one view will be necessary and sometimes a single three-dimensional drawing will be better. The important thing is that a working drawing **must** contain **all** the details which would enable someone else to make your design.

Whatever form of working drawing you do you should also include the following details:

- Specific names of materials used.
- The method of joining the parts together.
- The dimensions.
- The fittings (hinges, handles, catches, etc) which will be used.
- The type of finish to be applied.
- A list of parts.

Hints for production drawings

1 *Select a suitable way of showing all the information clearly*
2 *Others should be able to work from your drawings*
3 *Include all the details listed above*
4 *Drawings may need modification if work 'at the bench' shows a need for further refinement*
5 *Space the drawings out a little so that the sheet does not look cluttered*
6 *Use colour only where it is needed to make the drawing clearer*
7 *Orthographic drawings should be done according to British Standard PP7308*
8 *Add a list of parts*

Quality of communication

You are expected to communicate your ideas in a clear and appropriate way. Some communication will be in the form of models and mock-ups but the majority will be done on paper. For the highest marks you are expected to show a range of techniques appropriate to the task. A high level of precision should be shown and working drawings will generally need to comply with the relevant British Standard (usually PP7308). There is more information about this in Section Three.

> Up to
> **5** per cent
> of your marks

Planning and organization

This is a vague term and can include most parts of the design process but in particular you must be careful to plan the use of your time carefully. Of course CDT is not the only subject you are studying and you will need to be particularly well organized to get all your work done without wasting time and effort. Time is likely to be your greatest enemy in all parts of your coursework and so it is essential that you devise a scheme which will allow you to use your time effectively.

During the making phase of each project you can organize yourself best if you know what you intend to do.

> Up to
> **5** per cent
> of your marks

- Begin by producing a list of the tasks necessary to complete the project.
- List some of the problems which could occur.
- Try to arrange the list of tasks in a logical order.
- Include, where possible, alternative tasks if, say, machinery isn't available or materials have to be ordered.

Section Five shows examples of how to produce a plan for the manufacturing of your project. Do remember, for example, that glue needs time to set and painting will need a number of coats and so you will have to allow time for this. You should always go to a CDT lesson knowing what you intend to do. It is pointless to turn up and then spend a long time deciding what to do. Some people find that they are able to do practical work at home or at lunchtime but if you are not so fortunate do not waste the opportunities you have during practical lessons. Remember, design and planning work can usually be done at home.

Examiners will expect to find evidence that you have actually given **thought** and **time** to this activity and that you have not just left things to chance or merely kept things in the back of your mind. Further advice on these matters is given in Section Five.

Hints for planning the production of a project

1 *Planning will make life easier and save time*
2 *Plan to allow for things going wrong*
3 *Be realistic about how long things take*
4 *Provide evidence that you have given thought and time to planning*
5 *Ask for guidance from your teacher*

▶ Making skills (realization skills)

Up to
30 per cent of your marks

You are expected to be able to make the projects you have designed and all examination groups stipulate that you need experience in working in more than one material. It is not necessary to restrict yourself to timber, metals and plastics, although these are the materials usually available in schools. Materials such as concrete, paper products, modern composites and textiles are usually acceptable. Some projects may also require the use of electronic components.

When your work is assessed the following areas will be taken into account:

▶ Construction quality

Up to
7½ per cent of your marks

Examiners will expect to see a range of appropriate techniques applied to correctly selected materials and components. Materials should be selected with due regard to cost and properties and the manufacturing facilities available. You will be expected to show a good standard of workmanship. Components should be joined together with suitable and appropriate fixings and/or adhesives. The highest marks will go to those candidates whose work shows care and precision in the use of tools and equipment applied to sound constructional techniques.

▶ Accuracy

Up to
6 per cent of your marks

You are expected to manufacture your work accurately according to your drawings making modifications where necessary. Components must fit each other well. This is often best achieved by care and accuracy at the marking out stage, ensuring that the selected tools are in good condition, and a careful and methodical approach to manufacture. Machine-made components should show a high level of precision. It is often the case that products which are accurately made are those which work most efficiently.

▶ Finish

Up to
5 per cent of your marks

Materials should be smooth and even where appropriate. Marking out lines should be erased. Extreme sharp corners and edges should be removed. Your work is expected to have the appropriate surface finish which must be applied carefully so that the resulting appearance is of a high standard. You should take the necessary precautions to avoid unnecessary marking or damage to the surfaces during the process of manufacture.

Appearance

The appearance of your work should be such as to suit its function and the environment in which it is to be used. Candidates who pay too much attention to pleasing appearance in inappropriate circumstances are wasting time and effort.
Similarly where a candidate's work is expected to harmonize with its surroundings the candidate will not get the best marks if proper attention is not given to this aspect of appearance. Sensible and sensitive use of colour applied in the correct proportions is what is expected.

Safety

As you make your design your teacher will be checking that you work safely and may be awarding you marks for this. It is important that you obey all workroom rules and that you are particularly careful when using machines. LEAG award marks for safety during the 'design and make' examination. MEG award marks for safety as part of your coursework. Experience has shown that candidates who take care with safety as well as avoiding accidents also tend to produce work of a higher standard.

You should be particularly careful when manufacturing the project in a 'design and make' examination as you may feel under pressure and it is all too easy to rush.

Be careful to use the safety guards on machines and wear goggles or a visor when using machines or working with hot or hazardous materials.

If you ignore the safety rules you cannot expect to get a high mark for this part of the assessment.

The making part of your coursework can earn you more than half of your coursework marks. Section Seven gives further advice about making your projects.

Evaluation and testing

This is not always done well by candidates but it is **very** important. Good evaluation throughout a project can mean the difference between a good examination grade and a poor one and so it is worth spending time on.

Evaluation is a continuous process and should not all be left until after the project is made

Evaluation is a continuous process and throughout the design and making of a project you will be making design decisions. Make sure the examiner knows how you are thinking by adding notes to your drawings. Selecting the best idea, choosing the most suitable materials, and deciding upon a manufacturing process are part of the evaluation of a project. In addition to these decisions it is also important to test and appraise your project after the manufacturing is completed.

When making your evaluation you should be honest about what you did and didn't do. It is expected that you will have made mistakes, being honest about it and saying what you ought to have done will get you high marks. Similarly, your finished products are unlikely to satisfy the specification perfectly. However, a critical and careful analysis is likely to improve your marks and will help you to avoid making similar errors in your next project.

One way of evaluating a product is to ask yourself **and** answer the following questions:

- Does my project satisfy the brief and specification?
- What are the strengths and successes of my project?
- What are the weaknesses and failures of my project?
- What problems did I have with my project and how did I overcome them?

Be critical about how you would do a similar project differently next time. Ask yourself **and** answer the following questions:

- Did I use my time effectively?
- How would I do it differently next time?
- How can my design be improved?

You will need to test your project and the test results may need to be presented as a chart or graph. You may also need to produce drawings as part of the evaluation explaining potential improvements to your project.

Another way to provide a final evaluation is to list the points of your specification but rephrase them as questions and alongside answer these questions. The example below shows how this can be done for the 'first aid kit for a hiker' project.

1 Does the kit contain all the necessary medical kit?	Almost but there was not enough room for everything.
2 Is it small enough to be carried in the outside pocket of a day rucksack?	Yes, it fits in all rucksacks which I have tested.
3 Is it waterproof?	I have tested it with a hosepipe and the contents did not get wet. I also submerged it in the bath.
4 Does it have any sharp edges or corners?	It hasn't any sharp edges or corners but the catch sometimes gets caught on my rucksack.
5 Are there seperate compartments for the contents?	I decided they would not be necessary. To make seperate compartments would be fiddly. I did, however, find that it was difficult to get small items out without emptying everything onto the ground. Next time I will produce seperate sections for the most used items: scissors, safety pins and tweezers.

Fig. 2.14 Example of a final evaluation

There is an 'evaluation' checklist in Appendix 4 of this book.

A typical coursework project

Introduction

So many projects will begin with a need and end with a made product that it is useful to see the individual stages set out in a single chart. The process is not always exactly as the chart below shows and sometimes you will miss certain parts out or add others. However, if you follow the chart you are unlikely to miss too much out from each project.

6 Of course, a project can begin with a solution which doesn't work properly and needs to be improved 9

> **A project begins with a need and ends when the need has been achieved Everything you do will gain you credit Keep everything you do and make sure you get credit for it**

Seeing the whole picture

The chart below shows a typical coursework project. It is set out as if from your own point of view. There are references to the various sections in this book down the left hand side of the chart and references to checklists and other diagrammatic material down the right hand side. This material is to be found in Appendix 4. It is assumed that you will undertake three projects. Begin at the start and as you proceed with each project tick off each stage when you have completed it. When you consult a checklist or diagram you should tick this off also. All this will remind you of what you have done and what you still need to do.

A plan for a typical project

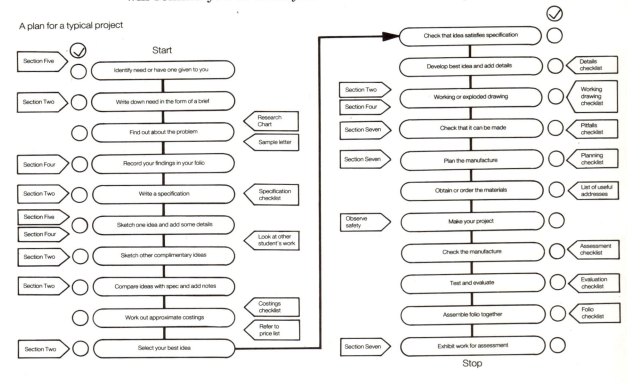

Communicating your ideas

Introduction

Throughout your course your teacher will insist that you communicate your ideas clearly. This may consist of explaining your thoughts to your teacher or friends or the making of models and mock-ups. Mostly, however, it will mean expressing your ideas on paper. Showing your ideas clearly is one of the most important parts of CDT. No matter how many good or even great ideas you have you will not do well in CDT if you cannot communicate them to others. In addition, recording your ideas on paper and as models will help you to decide which of those are the good ideas and which of those are not so good.

Putting your ideas on paper

Freehand drawing

You will be able to draw straight lines using a ruler or 'T' and set squares but it is also worth practising drawing them freehand otherwise you will find that you cannot put down your ideas quickly enough in a timed examination. It's surprising how easy it can be once you've mastered the basics.

● Think simple to begin with and get your drawings of 'straightforward' objects looking correct before you go on to drawing more complicated ones.

● Use a soft (2B) pencil and work faintly until you are sure the lines are in the correct place.

● When you are sure the lines are correct go over them to make them darker.

● Do not work with ink until you are confident with pencil.

To begin with, make sure you can draw vertical and horizontal lines. Sloping lines are less common and curves are often only a matter of rounding the edges where two straight lines meet. If your ultimate intention is to actually make the object you are drawing then you will 'find it easier to shape if it consists mostly of straight lines and simple curves. As a general rule if you find you have a lot of difficulty in drawing something you will also find that you will have difficulty in making it accurately.

When you are sure you can draw straight lines try drawing circles. A simple way of doing this is illustrated below.

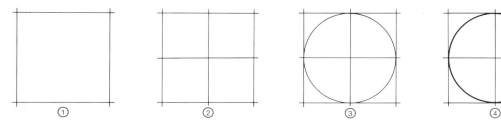

Fig. 4.1 Drawing circles

You will be able to draw many of your ideas using two dimensions but to give a true impression of your ideas you must try to draw in three dimensions. Fig. 4.2 shows you how to draw simple forms in three

Try drawing simple objects like these. It might help to begin with if you trace them **'**

dimensions. Two different styles of three-dimensional drawing are shown. Oblique/planometric is easier to draw but isometric often looks more realistic.

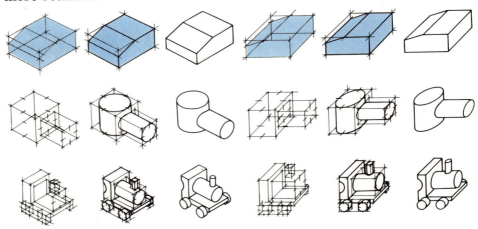

Fig. 4.2 Drawing in three dimensions can be easy

You may also know about perspective. If you do, use it if you think it gives more realistic drawings.

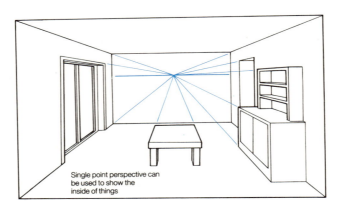

Single point perspective can be used to show the inside of things

' *This personal stereo was designed by a fifth year student and produced as a non-working model* **'**

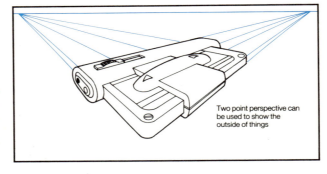

Two point perspective can be used to show the outside of things

Fig. 4.3 Perspective drawings

Make your ideas flow

Try to make your ideas flow naturally from one idea to the next. When you are developing an idea change details slowly so that you can judge if your new idea is an improvement on the previous one. Let the examiner see how your ideas have developed by linking them together. Using arrows can help. Fig. 4.4 shows how one student communicated the way she developed her idea.

Making drawings stand out

If you are particularly pleased with a drawing or you think it is your best idea you will want to make it stand out. The following techniques allow you to 'highlight' ideas on a page and draw the observer's attention to the one which is of particular interest. (Of course, if you apply these techniques to all your drawings the effect will be lost.)

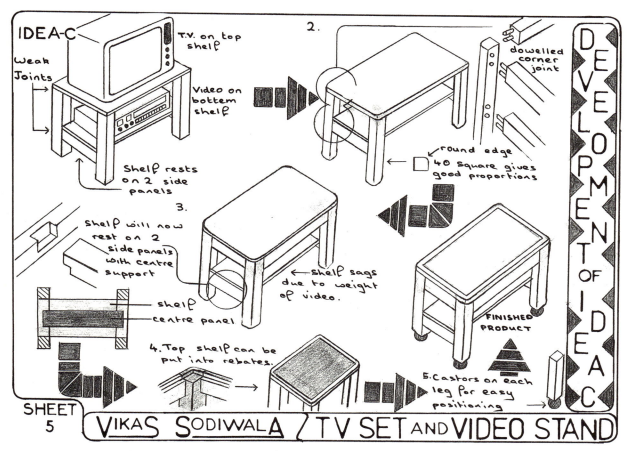

Fig. 4.4 Let your ideas flow

Thick and thin line

This technique is used a lot in illustrating books. A line represents the edge where two surfaces meet. The technique is simple. If you can see both surfaces draw a thin line. If you can only see one of the surfaces draw a thick one. It is most effective when done either with a 2H pencil (thin line) and 2B pencil (thick line) or using fine fibre or felt-tip pens or drawing pens.

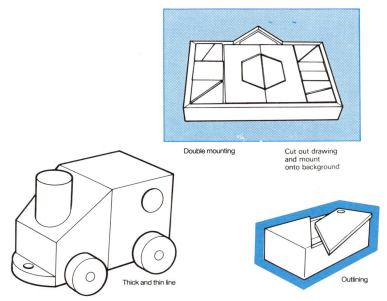

Fig. 4.5 Thick and thin line technique, outlining and double mounting

Colour shading

Imagine that light is shining from over your left shoulder (it doesn't really matter which direction you choose but over the left shoulder is as good as any):

- Leave the top surface white.
- Shade left hand verticals lightly and right hand verticals slightly heavier.
- Sloping surfaces will be somewhere in between. Notice how curves are done. Note the position of the highlight.
- If you decide to colour try to make the colour you use represent the colour you intend the finished object to be.
- You can also shade using ordinary pencils.

Outlining with a felt marker

The effect of outlining is to make your idea appear as if it is drawn against a coloured background. Use a broad felt marker, not fine-tipped pens. A similar effect can be achieved by double mounting although this may take longer to do.

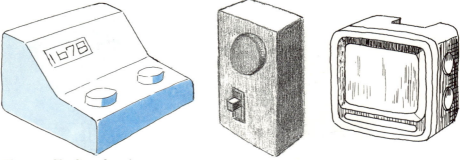

Fig. 4.6 Shading drawings

If you are drawing in ink then you may use a method which uses vertical lines of different spacing to give an illusion of shade.

Showing texture

Surface texture can be indicated on drawings. Do **you** think the textures shown on the following illustrations helps?

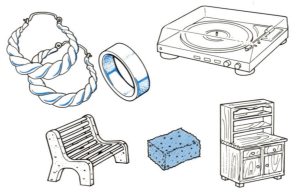

Fig. 4.7 Adding texture to drawings

What size should you make your drawings?

Full size if you can as it will make taking measurements easier. However, if you cannot do this you should always give some idea of the scale of your drawing. The importance of doing this is shown below.

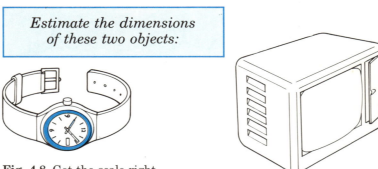

Estimate the dimensions of these two objects:

Fig. 4.8 Get the scale right

Fig. 4.9 Draw in a context

Got the idea? Give some clue as to real size—a hand, a door, an everyday object and consult the data sheets in Appendix 3.

How many drawings should there be on each sheet of paper?

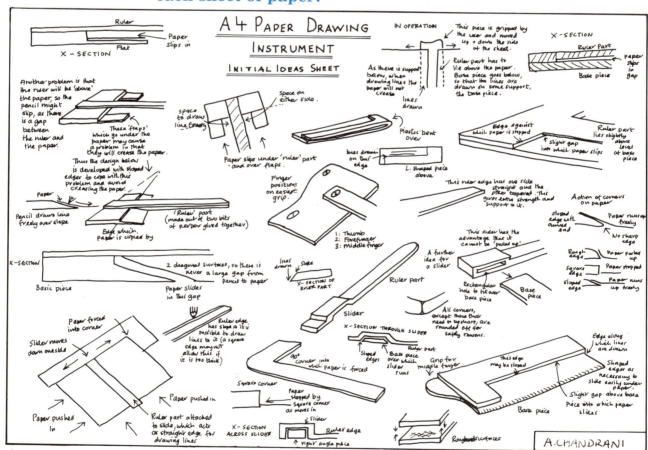

Fig. 4.10 Use your paper sensibly

Do you think the student has made a sensible use of the paper?

The question of how many drawings should there be on each sheet of paper is often asked by students and it is impossible to give an answer since drawings will be of different sizes. They will be drawn for different purposes and sheets of paper will vary. As a rough guide consider the following points:

1 Make sure each drawing is large enough to communicate or record what you intend but not so large as to waste space.

2 Arrange your drawings on the paper so that there is a little space between them and the sheet does not look cluttered.

3 Do not waste paper by putting a single drawing in the centre with lots of space all around.

Lettering and writing

Adding notes to ideas is very important but it can present difficulties if your handwriting is not very good. To improve this:

- Make sure the written lines are horizontal.
- Use faint guidelines to assist.
- Write small and keep your writing to a minimum.
- Brief notes are all that is usually required.
- You can add lettering by hand or you can use stencils.
- For your final presentation and working drawings you may like to use rub down letters such as 'Letraset'.
- Headings and section titles ('Problem', 'Design brief', 'Analysis', etc,) can be produced on a computer, run out and pasted on. These can look very effective if mounted on a coloured background.
- If you need to put the same words, etc, on a number of different sheets (the project title, for example) write them down carefully or use rub down letters and then photocopy a number of times and paste onto the relevant sheets.

There are lots of other ways of lettering. Whatever you do make it clear and readable

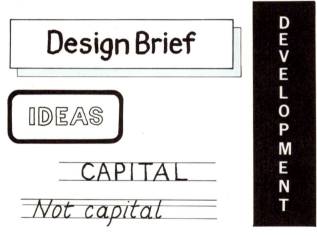

Fig. 4.11 Lettering styles

Orthographic drawings

Orthographic drawings are usually done for your final or working drawing.

- Draw clearly, usually with instruments.
- Use the appropriate British Standard (usually PP7308).
- Add a cutting or parts list.
- Add dimensions and details of materials.

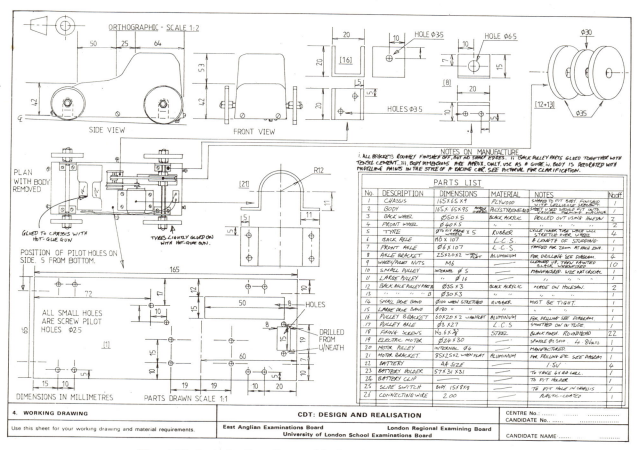

Fig. 4.12 A student's orthographic drawing

Computer-aided drawing

The increasing use of computers and the availability of graphics software makes it possible to produce a wide variety of drawings using a computer. The software presently available for school use and the types of computer in many schools are not really suitable for putting down your initial ideas. You can, however, produce the working drawing of your project if the project is not too complicated. Computer-aided drawing can also be used to draw charts and diagrams (see Fig. 4.13).

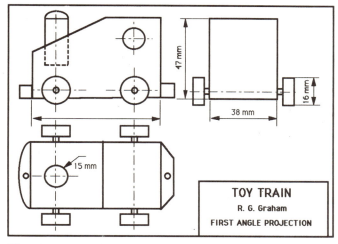

Fig. 4.13 A production drawing produced on the Apple Macintosh using 'Macdraw'

Using isometric grids

Isometric grid paper can be a useful way to produce three-dimensional drawings and one examination group actually provides some for use in the design examination. Sometimes you can get a better looking result by putting the grid onto a light box or even a light-coloured surface, placing plain white paper on top and using the grid as a guide. The following example shows how a student has used isometric grid paper.

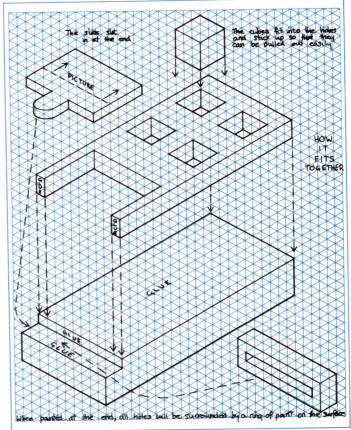

Fig. 4.14 Using isometric grid paper

If you haven't got a light box you can obtain a similar effect by holding the drawings up against a window.

Exploded drawings

Exploded drawings can be an excellent way of showing how a product is assembled. Use isometric grid paper to help.

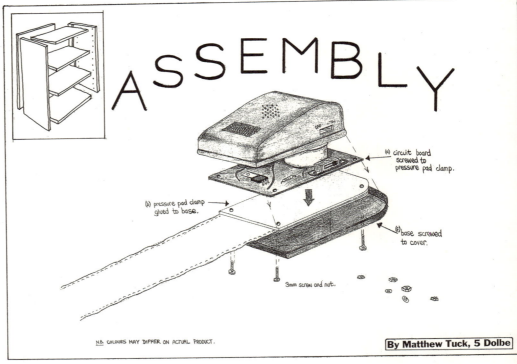

Fig. 4.15 Exploded drawings

Models and mock-ups

You may need to model your design. Models are made for different reasons:

- To communicate an idea which cannot easily be done with a drawing, e.g. a free or organic shape such as a carving or a piece of pottery or jewellery.

- To illustrate how a moving system works, e.g. card linkages or a model made from Lego or Fischertechnic.

- Where it is necessary to explore how two or more parts fit together.

- When investigating the layout of parts of a project, in particular when making ergonomic considerations.

- Where full size would be impractical.

'Models or mock-ups are often a better way of developing an idea than a drawing'

Depending upon the function of the model you will use different materials. Here is a list of some which could be useful:

1. Paper, card.
2. Polystyrene sheet.
3. Expanded polystyrene/polyurethane, styrofoam.
4. Balsa wood.
5. Plasticine, clay.
6. Wire.
7. Meccanno, Fischertechnic, Lego.

The following photographs illustrate some examples of the models which you might need to make.

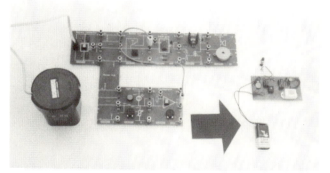

Fig. 4.16 Models can help the design process

Photographs

These can be very effective in showing your work as it progresses and to show the finished product. Photographs are particularly useful if your work has to be sent away for assessment. Sometimes models and mock-ups cannot be kept (others may need to use the Meccanno pieces, for example), and in these cases you will need to supply a photograph to show an assessor what you did. However, photographs are of very little use unless they show clearly what you want them to show. A few

simple rules may help you to take better photographs. The rules are:
- Make sure the photograph is big enough. Use a close-up lens if necessary.
- Make sure that the photograph is in focus.
- Make sure there is enough light so that only a small aperture is needed.
- Take photographs from different angles but only put the best ones in your design folio.
- Try to arrange a plain background for your photographs (a large piece of paper, a bedsheet or a large piece of felt can be effective).

Include in the photograph an object, for example, coin, ruler or hand, to give an idea of scale.

Presenting research information

Whatever research you do you will want to show what you have done. You must present it in your folio in such a way that the examiner can see how much effort you have made.

Primary research

Primary research includes experiments, tests, questionnaires, interviews and surveys. Results of experiments, tests and surveys can be presented as follows:

1 As tables of results.
2 As graphs, pie charts, bar charts.
3 As photographs of experiments.

Answers to interviews, questionnaires and surveys can be presented as follows:

1 As tables of results.
2 As a photograph of an interview or situation.
3 As videos, tape recordings.

Conclusions drawn from questionnaires can be presented as follows:

1 As tables of results.
2 As graphs.

There are lots of other ways you can use computers to present your work

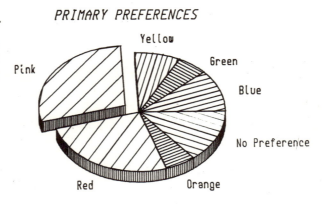
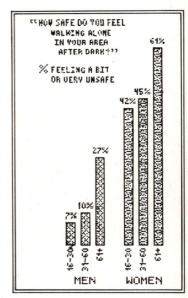

Fig. 4.17 Primary research presented by charts prepared using a computer

Secondary research

Press cuttings and photocopies can be presented as follows:

1 By pasting in, by double mounting.

2 By adding notes and comments.

Replies to letters can be presented as follows:
1 By pasting in.
2 By highlighting the relevant information.
3 By adding comments on the value of the information.

Technical data from books and charts can be presented as follows:
1 By pasting in photocopies.
2 By highlighting the parts which matter to the project.

Photographs and photocopies can be presented as follows:
1 By pasting in.
2 By acknowledging the source and giving reasons for inclusion in the project.

Using catalogue illustrations

Cuttings from catalogues (mail order, brochures, etc) should be used with caution. They should not be used to merely fill out a project folder. Any catalogue cutting must be accompanied by a written commentary, indicating:

1 Source of the illustration.
2 Strengths and weaknesses of the ideas illustrated.
3 Possible ideas for improvements.

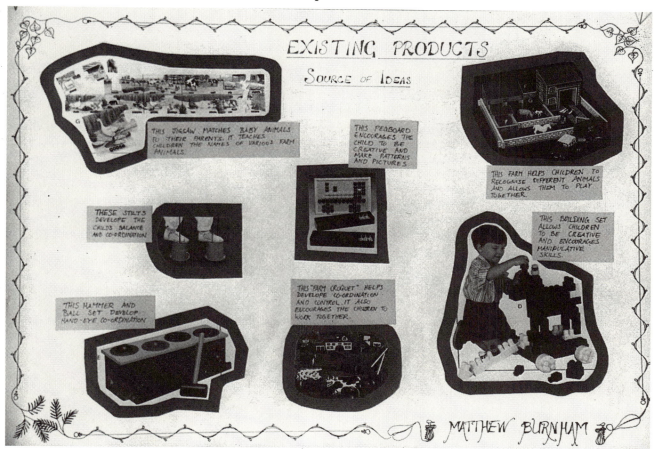

Fig. 4.18 Presenting secondary research

Using photocopiers

Using photocopiers can assist you in presenting your ideas. For example, you can:
- Make copies of an original and experiment with different colours.
- Enlarge or reduce drawings.
- Cut up drawings, paste in new positions and photocopy.
- Copy photographs and illustrations and colour with markers.
- Produce copies of logos or headings.

Personalizing your work

It will help to give a good impression to the examiner if your work shows 'individual' touches. You could, for example:

- Adopt a personal colour scheme.
- Make sure all project folios have contents pages which are produced in the same style.
- Use a personal logo (possibly produced on a computer and photocopied) which could be added to all your drawing sheets (say at the bottom right hand corner).
- Make sure all labels are produced in the same style.

Mistakes

You are likely to make mistakes in your folio. The following advice may be of help to you:

- Redrawing the corrected text or diagram on a separate piece of paper and pasting this over the original mistake.
- You may also double mount your work by pasting on a piece of paper of a different colour and then pasting onto the main sheet.
- Try to avoid crossing out and overuse of correction fluid (Tippex) should be avoided as it does not look very attractive.
- Drawing with faint lines until your drawing looks correct and then 'lining in' with a heavier pencil will avoid too many untidy errors.

But what if you still can't draw?

- Try using tracing paper to trace over your initial ideas.
- Trace ideas from books and using more tracing paper make changes.
- Don't worry about putting all your drawings on a single sheet. You can always mount them later.
- However poor your drawing get your ideas down before you forget them.
- Photograph objects and copy the drawings.
- Use a video camera and trace the image directly from the TV screen.
- Photocopy ideas, cut and paste, then photocopy again.
- Photocopy onto an acetate sheet. Project with an overhead projector and trace from the projector image.
- Use an optical scanner with a microcomputer. Change the shape and proportions of the drawing, add the finer details and then print out.

'Not everyone finds it easy to draw. Try these ideas. They may help'

Gaining more space on the paper

This can be achieved by the use of fold out flaps, pockets and by folding illustrations. Fig. 4.19 shows examples of this.

Similarly the use of overlays can help communicate how an idea has developed or show different levels such as would be necessary for the design of a building or a three-dimensional maze.

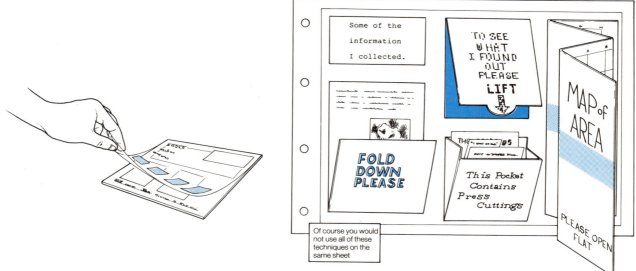

Fig. 4.19 Gaining additional space on the paper

You are advised to use these techniques with caution as they can spoil a folio if they are overdone. Do not use more than one technique on the same sheet and make sure they are secure and there is no danger of parts falling from your project or becoming damaged as the folio is handled.

Hints for communicating ideas on paper

1 *Think simple to begin with*
2 *Don't overdo shading and highlighting techniques*
3 *If possible, keep ideas on one topic or theme on the same sheet*
4 *Computer-aided drawing is effective for some production drawings*
5 *Isometric grid paper can help for some drawings but for best results use the grid as a guide and draw on plain white paper using a light box or a window*
6 *Leave a small space between your drawings so that sheets do not appear cluttered, but don't make the spaces too large or it will simply look as though you are trying to use up paper*
7 *Make your ideas flow so the examiner can see how your idea developed*
8 *Do not draw in ink or felt pen unless you are experienced in using them. It is better to use pencil and add colour with coloured pencils*
9 *Leave a small space around the edges of each sheet to act as a border. Alternatively draw a border about 10mm wide (a little wider where the folder is to be bound)*

Hints for making models

1 *Make models when they are needed*
2 *Do not make them more complicated than they need to be*
3 *Keep models or take photographs of them if they have to be taken apart again*

Starting your projects

Introduction

All examination groups award a high proportion of marks to coursework and so it is important you do it well and get on with it straight away. When you start a project you are likely to be given a brief or theme or you will have to decide one for yourself. Being given a brief can often be easier but it gives you less chance to tackle a project in which you may have a particular interest.

You must choose your projects carefully so that you can do your best work, develop your understanding and perhaps, most importantly, earn the best credit in the examination. Examination groups often say that the best marks will go to those candidates who are able to identify their own problems. In other words, if you always have to ask your teacher what to do then you are not likely to gain a very high grade. Your teacher will, of course, advise and help you to avoid too many pitfalls, such as tackling a project for which it will be impossible to find the resources or which will take too long, but will encourage you to identify problems, needs and tasks yourself. The world is full of problems just waiting to be solved. Solving them can be the easy part. Seeing they are there is the difficult part.

Types of project

Before you begin thinking about projects it may be helpful to see examples of how other students have worked.

Inventing something completely new

Inventing something completely new is very rare

You might be lucky enough to come up with a completely new idea and if you do it could make you your fortune. Just occasionally you will find yourself trying to do a job where you need a special piece of equipment and the only thing you can do is design and make it yourself. Very probably it will only be a simple device, but if it's not been thought of before and there is a need for it, you could become very wealthy! For example, about twenty years ago a person invented a portable folding bench. He had difficulty persuading any manufacturer to take the idea seriously since no one had ever seen anything like it before. Black and Decker eventually took the idea and since then more than thirty million 'Workmates' have been sold.

If you have ever seen beer being brewed at home then you will know that it has to be siphoned out of the fermenting vessel. It's an awkward job and if you let go of the siphon tube it either drops into the vessel and sucks up the 'mash' from the bottom or the weight of the tube causes it to be pulled out of the vessel. To get over this some home brewers used a bulldog clip but this was difficult to clean and if it fell into the beer it could make the beer taste odd. One student improved on this by producing the clip shown in Fig. 5.1. Some years later a similar product was manufactured commercially and was sold in a well-known chain store.

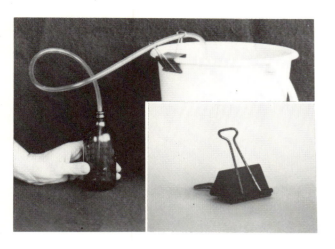 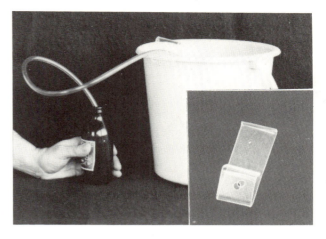

NOW CAN YOU SUGGEST A FURTHER IMPROVEMENT?

_____

_____

_____

_____

_____

_____

_____

Fig. 5.1 The invention of a new idea

Have a look at the photograph of the clip above. Could you improve it even further?

Working as a group

Some students find it helpful to work as a member of a group. This can have the advantage of allowing you to tackle a bigger project. Group projects also allow each individual to contribute their own skills whilst at the same time benefiting from those of others.

If you are thinking of a group project you will have to consider the following:

● Can the project be divided into sufficient parts or tasks to enable each member of the team to be responsible for one task (or a group of tasks)?

● Can the project be planned so that all members of the group will be employed throughout the project?

● Are you all sure that you all want to undertake this project?

● Are you willing to make an equal contribution of effort?

● Have you carefully thought through the problems you may face?

● What will you do if one member of the group loses interest?

● How will you record the contributions made by each member so that the work can be assessed (for the examination)?

● Who will be the 'owner' when the project is completed?

Which of these projects could you develop as a group project?

1 Toys for a children's play group?
2 Garden seating?
3 A computer workstation?

Working as a cooperative

On page 49 you can see details of an airbrush designed by a student. What other pieces of equipment could be designed to go alongside the airbrush?

Can you add others to this diagram?

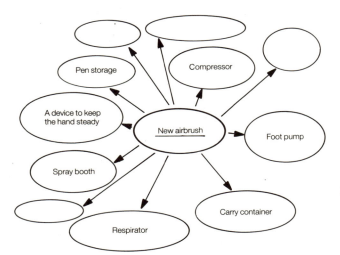

Fig. 5.2 Cooperative working

Could you organize yourself and your friends to design and make a complete airbrush 'kit'?

A mini-enterprise project

Working as a group or individually you could get involved in a product with commercial potential. A group from one school produced a recording of music. They designed the sleeve for the tape and the packaging, organized the publicity and made some profit which they donated to charity.

Another group 'designed' chocolate bars. They worked out the nutritional value, tried out their ideas on friends, market researched the shape and taste, then made the mould for the chocolate, designed the packaging and organized the manufacture and sold the product at a school fête. The profits (such as they were) were then used to fund their next enterprise.

Have you any ideas which have commercial potential? Can you design for a school fête? And what about promoting the interests of your school? If you're proud of it let the world know!

Remember, you might be willing to buy it but will others? You may need to do some market research

Try listing as many ideas as you can of things you think would sell. Here's a start:

1 *Badges and buttons* ....
2 *Personalized pencil cases* ....

3 Shopping bags ....

4 Boxes of sweets ....

5 ....

6 ....

7 ....

8 ....

Do something to benefit a local group

Many students give up some of their spare time to work with
'community groups'. They may help in a local hospital, give assistance
at a children's nursery, visit elderly people living alone or raise money
for a local charity by running sponsored events or helping with door to
door collections. One student helped in a home for elderly people where
her aunt was matron. She noticed that some of the residents were
having difficulty when trying to lift themselves out of their armchairs.
The residents said that the difficulty was that they hadn't the strength
to push up on the arms of their chairs. They had been offered a 'grab'
rail which was to be fixed above the seat suspended from the ceiling
but this would mean that the chairs couldn't be moved. Matron felt
that such 'grab' rails would also make the lounge look too much like a
hospital. This situation provided a starting point for a CDT project. The
student tackled the problem with enthusiasm and some of her design
work is shown later in this book. The finished product turned out to be
more complicated than she expected and is shown below. It consists of a
rising wooden seat operated by compressed air from a cheap electrical
compressor.

*The project analysis
and some of the
research for this
project can be seen
in Fig. 6.7.
An evaluation can
be seen in Fig. 6.18*

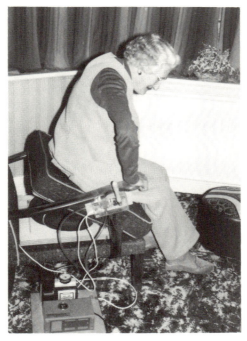

Fig. 5.3 A student's contribution to an elderly persons' home

Enter for a design competition

Frequently your teacher is sent details of design competitions which
are run on a national and local basis. You may see details of these
advertised on school noticeboards and sometimes in public libraries. If
you want to enter one you can usually submit your entry as part of
your CDT coursework. You may already be working on a project which
would be suitable without alteration for entry for the competition. It
can do no harm to enter and you may do well and bring credit to
yourself and your school.

Fig. 5.4 There are lots of competitions to enter

Choose something which interests you

You can list your interests or show them in a chart like the one below and this can help you to find a topic for a project.

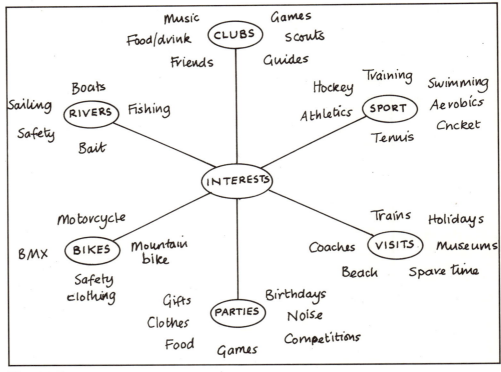

Fig. 5.5 Interests

One student developed the idea of personal interests further and expanded on the topic of games and sports. The different sports were listed as a number of headings. Athletics was further identified and then a particular event: the long jump. The student remembered the difficulty faced with deciding if a jump was a foul. Finally an automatic 'foul jump indicator' was designed. It was a fairly simple affair. It replaced the existing take off board, had a pressure sensitive strip at the edge and this switched on a light if the athlete's toe was over the edge of the board.

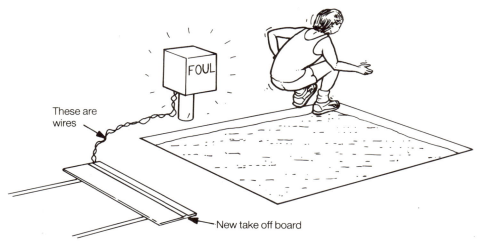

These are wires

New take off board

Fig. 5.6 'Foul jump indicator'

Consider your own qualities

A useful way to make sure your project interests you and is within your ability is to remind yourself of your personal qualities and interests.

Here are two self-check lists. Tick the statements which apply to you

Personal qualities and interests		Tick the appropriate boxes (√)				
I prefer to work on:	Artistic projects		Technology projects		A mixture of the two	
I like working:	Alone		With a partner		As a team member	
I like making:	Large projects		Average size projects		Small projects	
I like making things which:	Work		Have working parts		Have no working parts	
I like to learn:	New processes		New processes when necessary		Prefer to stick with what I already know	

Fig. 5.7a Consider your qualities and interests

CDT experience		Tick the appropriate boxes (√)				
I can use:	Most hand tools		Tools for one material only		Only a few tools	
I can use:	Most CDT machinery		Machinery for one material only		Only one or two machines	
I have worked:	In a range of materials		Mainly in one material		Only in one material	
In my projects I have included:	Technology		A little technology		No technology	
	Information technology		A little information technology		No information technology	

cont'd

CDT skills	*Tick the appropriate boxes* (√)					
I find writing a design brief and specification:		Easy		Average		Difficult
I find analysing problems:		Easy		Easy with help		Difficult
I find planning:		Easy		Average		Difficult
My graphics skills are:		Very good		Good		Below average
I find working without constant help:		Easy		Quite easy		Difficult
The quality of finish of my work is:		Very high		Average		Rather poor
I find evaluating my work:		Easy		Fairly easy		Difficult

Special talents	*Tick the appropriate boxes* (√)					
I am able to work:		Quickly		Average speed		Slowly
		Very carefully		Carefully		Slapdash
		Accurately		Fairly accurately		Not accurately
I can:		Easily get my own materials		Get some of my own materials		Expect my teacher to provide them all
I like to do my CDT:		At school and at home		At school		At home
When researching a project:		I enjoy it		Do it		Hate it

Fig. 5.7b Consider your skills, experience and special talents

After completing these charts you will find it helpful to discuss them with your teacher.

Fig. 5.8 shows an extract from a chart completed by a fourth year student. The student was deciding which project to tackle. Look at the things which the student is good at and try to decide which project would be most suitable. This is the beginning of the CDT course and so a project which is successful is very important

The student has proposed the following as possible projects:

1 Furniture for a baby sister's doll's house.
2 A lock for the student's tandem (cycle) which is used with a friend at weekends and during the school holidays.
3 A climbing frame for the garden.

The checklist should help to decide which project is most suitable.

CDT experience	*Tick the appropriate boxes* (√)					
I can use:		Most hand tools		Tools for one material only	√	Only a few tools
I can use:		Machinery for one material only			√	Only one or two machines
	√	Mainly in one material				Only in one material
		A little technology				No technology
		A little information technology				No information technology

Personal qualities and interests	*Tick the appropriate boxes* (√)					
I prefer to work on:		Artistic projects		Technology projects		A mixture of the two
I like working:	√	Alone		With a partner		As a team member
I like making:		Large projects		Average size projects	√	Small projects
I like making things which:		Work		Have working parts	√	Have no working parts
I like to learn:		New processes	√	New processes when necessary		Prefer to stick with what I already know

CDT skills   *Tick the appropriate boxes (√)*

I find writing a design brief and specification:	Easy	✓ Average	Difficult
I find analysing problems:	✓ Easy	Easy with help	Difficult
I find planning:	Easy	✓ Average	Difficult
My graphics skills are:	Very good	Good	✓ Below average
I find working without constant help:	✓ Easy	Quite easy	Difficult
The quality of my work is:			Rather poor
I find evaluat...			

Special talents   *Tick the appropriate boxes (√)*

I am able to work:	Quickly	✓ Average speed	Slowly
	Very carefully	✓ Carefully	Slapdash
I can:	✓ Accurately	Fairly accurately	Not accurately
I like to do my CDT:	Easily get my own materials	✓ Get some of my own materials	Expect my teacher to provide them all
When researching a project	✓ At school and at home	At school	At home
	I enjoy it	✓ Do it	Hate it

Fig. 5.8 How the student filled in the checklist

We see that the student prefers to make small items and so this rules out the climbing frame. The student prefers to work alone and this would make either of the other projects suitable. Other skills may be needed for both remaining projects, but we see a willingness to learn others when necessary. Accuracy and care will be particularly important with the locking mechanism and it is certain to need technology and have working parts. Additionally a willingness to work at home will be necessary for the locking mechanism as it will not be easy to bring the tandem to school too frequently. The incentive of a personal need will also spur this student on to complete it on time.

The student decided to tackle the locking mechanism and now is much more certain that no one will steal the tandem when it is left unattended.

Observe situations

If you keep your eyes open you will very often see things which are not being done as well as they might and this may enable you to gain an idea for a project that will improve or solve the situation or problem.

Some scenarios include:

1 People using too much energy.
2 Materials being wasted.
3 Operations which are not as safe as they might be.
4 Things being left in an untidy state.
5 Rubbish being blown around the streets.

The illustration on the next page, for example, shows things not being done the way they should be in the CDT room at school.

Fig. 5.9 Dangers in school

> *Identify the dangers in this drawing. They can be grouped into different types. See if you can list them under the following headings:*

Dangers with heat	Dangers with chemicals
1 _____	1 _____
2 _____	2 _____
3 _____	3 _____
4 _____	4 _____
5 _____	5 _____
Dangers with cutting	**Electrical dangers**
1 _____	1 _____
2 _____	2 _____
3 _____	3 _____
4 _____	4 _____
5 _____	5 _____

Fig. 5.10 Categorizing the dangers

Improve existing products

Whenever you use anything ask yourself 'Is this doing the job as well as it should?' If the answer is 'No', then make a note of your discovery in your CDT diary (more of this later), your CDT notebook or your CDT exercise book. This way you will gather a number of possible starting points for projects in the future. One student, for example, noticed that airbrushes were difficult to clean and that the only solution was a brush made by 'Letterajet' which used an expensive felt marker as the source of ink. This student, therefore, designed an airbrush which could use any size of felt pen. And he always used the cheapest he could find.

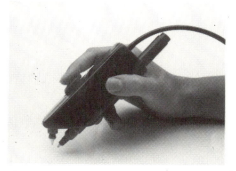

Fig. 5.11 Student improved airbrush

Analyse an existing project

Take any object which is familiar to you and consider changes that could be made to it or attachments which you could design.

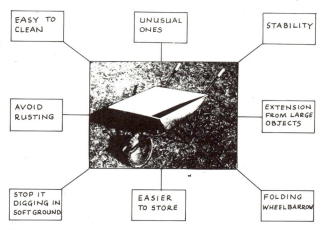

EASY TO CLEAN

UNUSUAL ONES

STABILITY

AVOID RUSTING

EXTENSION FROM LARGE OBJECTS

STOP IT DIGGING IN SOFT GROUND

EASIER TO STORE

FOLDING WHEELBARROW

Fig. 5.12 Analyse an existing product

> *What accessories could you design for this?*
> *Fill in the boxes with ideas*

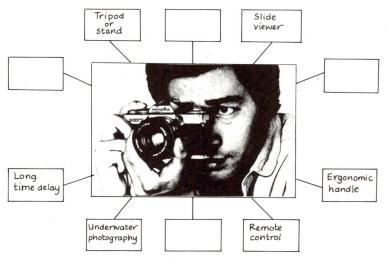

Tripod or stand

Slide viewer

Long time delay

Ergonomic handle

Underwater photography

Remote control

Fig. 5.13 Have a go at deciding on accessories and attachments

Analyse a situation

> *Have a look at Fig. 5.14 overleaf. What could you use the space for? Would you need to design extras?*

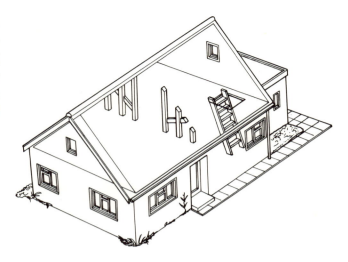

Fig. 5.14 A space waiting to be used

Try to add to the chart below your own ideas:

Possible uses	Things which might be needed
Store room	Shelving, books, sign for door

Fig. 5.15 Compiling your own ideas

Consider your previous experience

Try to broaden your experience. All examination groups require you to have experience in working with more than one material. As your course progresses you could find that your experience has been limited to only one main material or a small range of techniques. You must make sure that you widen your experience and a different material is incorporated into one of your projects. You will often be advised not to consider materials until the problem is clearly identified, analysed and a brief and specification written. This is very good advice but if you find yourself in the position of **having** to work in a different material then there are a few things which you can do to try to help identify a suitable problem.

Imagine you need to work in timber:

Certain types of project lend themselves to solutions made in timber. You could look at your home. In particular you could try to identify areas where things need to be tidier or better organized. This may lead to the design of some form of container or small piece of furniture.

Imagine you need to work in plastics:

As plastics are fairly hygienic and easily cleaned as well as not easily affected by hot water, you could look in the bathroom or kitchen. You are likely to see needs which could be made in plastics.

50

Imagine you need to work in metals:

Metals are usually, by their nature, strong and durable. They lend themselves to situations where objects may be subject to bangs and knocks and particularly where their strengths are needed. If you have a motorcycle or help with the repairs to the family car you may find that specialist tools or simple jigs, cramps or attachments are needed. Alternatively, if you are aesthetically inclined you could tackle a jewellery project in metal.

Starting the project

Fig. 5.16 Getting started may not be easy

Briefs may be chosen by the teacher, the topic of some competition or simply set by the examination group. Whatever the source of the brief there are a variety of ways you can make a start.

Try sharing your ideas with others

A simple and easy way to do this is by 'brainstorming'.

> *The scribe does not contribute to the discussion*

Fig. 5.17 A brainstorming session

Arrange for a group of friends or classmates to sit around a large table, clear the table from any distractions and appoint one person as 'scribe'. His (or her) task will be to write down the ideas which everyone has. It is important that the scribe does not contribute ideas or they may miss something suggested by others. Begin with a topic, problem or theme and allow all members of the group to call out ideas. The scribe writes them down as quickly as possible, either on a notepad or on the chalkboard. After a few minutes there may be as many as twenty or thirty ideas. Some may not seem directly connected to the theme but they will certainly give you ideas of topics which you can think about.

For example, one group asked to brainstorm the topic 'Security' came up with this list:

> Alarm – Lock – Insurance – Keys – Bank – Money – Safe – Paper – Combination – Burglary – Robber – Man – Woman – Child – Birth – Embryo – Social – Abortion – Death – Weapons – Guns – War – Ammunition – President Bush – NATO – Star Wars – Warsaw Pact – Gadaffi – Rushdie – Moslem – Faith – Belief – Hiding Place – The Hobbitt – Tolkein – Boots, ...

Fig. 5.18 The results of a brainstorming session

As this point the session was stopped as the topics had moved quite a long way from the original 'Security'. It is interesting to see, however, that topics which you certainly would not have expected were mentioned: 'Moslem', 'Abortion', 'Books'. One student was stimulated to develop a project about locks and another to design a personal alarm (some details of which are shown on page 34. One student thought it could be interesting to develop this session further and the group brainstormed the topic of 'Babies'. It resulted in the development of a set of kitchen scales!

Babies - Birth - Embryo - Reproduction - Life - Contraception - Clinic - NHS - BUPA - Flowers - Fertilization - Hospitals - Doctors - Nurses - Surgeons - Midwife - Family - Post Natal Clinic - Babycare - Child weight - Scales . . . .

Fig. 5.19 Brainstorming 'Babies'

Form yourselves into a group of four or five. Sit at a table. Sit the 'scribe' separately. Here are some topics to consider:

1 Animals.
2 Wide-open spaces.
3 Using spare time.
4 Recycling rubbish.
5 Packaging.
6 School holidays.
7 Birthdays.
8 Music.

Try making lists

Another approach which can help is to write down a list of all the important points in a topic. You can show this in the form of a 'bubble chart' or 'spidergram' and then add to each topic further sub-topics. This will help you to think generally about the problem. For example, in 1989 one examination group set the theme of 'childrens' learning toys' and so a student made a list of the important points (as the student saw them) and expressed them in the chart reproduced below. It may not be a very orthodox way to write a list but it does show how his thoughts developed – one thought triggering off another.

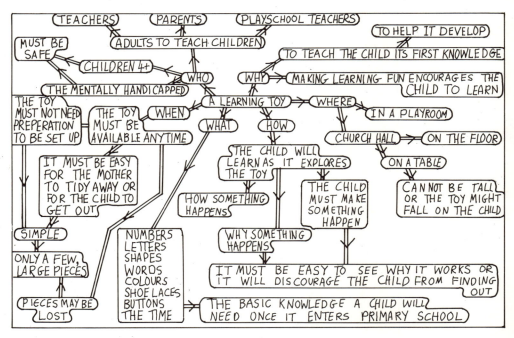

Fig. 5.20 A candidate's thought processes list

The student could equally well have begun with a number of headings and worked down the page like this:

CHILDREN	LEARNING	PLACES	SAFETY	EASE OF USE	FUN
Hand size	Alphabet	Play school	Non-toxic	Simple	Colourful
Strength	Numbers	Home	Rounded	Sizes	movement
	Shapes	Table	No corners	Number of pieces	Noise
Handicap	Words	Church Hall	Not heavy		Activity
Teachers	Shoelaces	Playroom	No loose bits	Simple rules	Not boring
	Time				

Fig. 5.21 Thinking in 'columns'

> *Consider the topic of 'storing food'. Working on a single A4 sheet try to put down your thoughts in either a bubble chart or in columns. In Fig. 5.22 below are suggestions of things you might have included. Cover it up so that you can try this exercise yourself before looking. Spend about five minutes on this task*

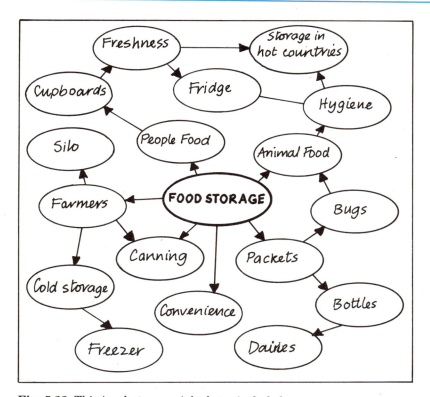

Fig. 5.22 This is what you might have included

You will probably have missed some of the points mentioned above. Ask yourself why you missed the points. Did you get stuck in a rut and fail to think widely? For example, did you only think of human food? Or did you restrict yourself to thinking only of food available in your home? If you think you are getting in a rut, stop, remind yourself of the starting point and you may then continue in a different direction.

Planning ahead

Time is never on your side and if you are to do well in a project you will need to be organized. You will need to:

● Know what you intend to do.

● Record what you actually do.

● Check that what you have done is what you intended to do.

- Decide what changes you now need to make.
- Modify your plan for the future.

Everyone finds it difficult to estimate how long things will take and there are always unforeseen circumstances. However, examiners realize the difficulties and will reward you for the efforts you make to overcome the problems you have. The secret is to realize that everything must be packed into a limited amount of time and however impossible the task may seem you must adjust your plans to make it possible. You can, for example, simplify the construction, produce one fewer drawing and above all, whilst trying to do your best, do not always strive for perfection! Getting the project completed may sometimes be much better than spending all your time planning how to make it perfect although incomplete projects will be marked and you will gain credit for them.

Planning your work

The first piece of information you will need is the date when each project has to be completed. Some projects may be done in a few weeks, others could last up to 12 months. However long the project is supposed to take, do not underestimate the importance of completing it on time. Begin by dividing your overall project time into smaller units of time. The two major parts are **designing** and **making**. Each is of equal importance although making usually takes longer than designing.

For example, if you suppose you have a 12 week project then your designing time could be divided as follows:

1 Identify need and write design brief	1 week
2 Analysis	1 week
3 Research	1 week
4 Development of ideas	1 week
5 Working drawing	1 week

The seven weeks allowed for making could be divided as follows:

1 Preparing materials	1 week
2 Marking out	1 week
3 Making of parts	3 weeks
4 Assembly	1 week
5 Cleaning and applying finish	1 week

However, when planning your work remember that it may work out exactly as you expect – but it usually will not! So what you need to know is how to prepare for and how to deal with things that go wrong.

Planning schedules

A planning schedule can be of help to you.

One method of setting out your planning is shown in Fig. 5.23. The project was undertaken for a two term period although most projects will usually be shorter. The chart shows that time has been allowed for each stage of the project. The blocks coloured black show the amount of time the candidate expected each task to take and when he or she expected to do it. The blocks shaded blue show what actually happened. Why do you think the candidate has shaded a blue block for evaluation during early November? And as the project deadline was set for the end of April why do you think the candidate has shown nothing planned to be done in April?

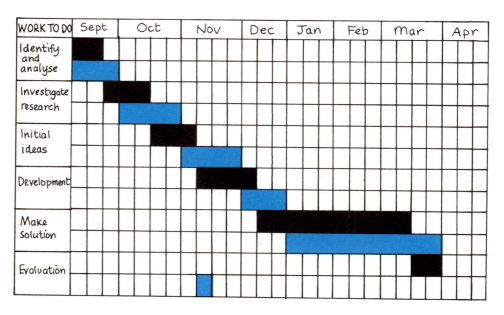

Fig. 5.23 A planning schedule

Keeping a diary

You can write down your intention in a pocket diary and this will enable you to think ahead but to be really effective a diary for CDT needs to:

Diaries help you plan the use of your time

1 Allow you to plan ahead.
2 Keep a record of what you did.
3 Allow you to avoid unnecessary wasted time.

> *A student made the following entry in a diary. Do you think it shows planning? Is it keeping a record? Will it help to avoid wasting time?*

Monday 23rd November

Made the lid of my box today. I don't know what to do next lesson because the hinges I ordered have not arrived.

Fig. 5.24 Keeping a diary

> *What do you think the student could do next? Give two activities which the student needs to plan*

1 ....

2 ....

Producing a planning schedule

You will need to know the following:
- What tasks you are going to perform.
- The order in which they will be done.
- Possible alternative tasks should equipment and resources not be available.
- An estimate of how long each task will take.

What tasks are you going to perform?

This will differ with each project but broadly speaking the ones shown in the 'Planning your work' section on page 54 will be included in most projects.

In which order will the tasks be performed?

The order of your tasks will broadly follow those shown in Fig. 5.23 but you may need to jump around a bit as you find you need more information or an idea requires more refinement before you can decide whether to reject or accept it.

What possible alternative tasks are there?

'Always have alternative tasks in mind'

Remember that equipment is shared with others in the class and materials may need to be specially ordered and may not arrive when you expect them. So always have alternative tasks in hand. You may not be able to predict too far ahead what alternative task to do, but do predict **in advance** even if it is only the night before your lesson. Bear in mind that what you intend to do in a lesson might not be possible, others, for example, may be using the machine that you need, so have an alternative task ready or make sure you get to the lesson first!

How long will each task take?

Consider the following:

- Tasks, particularly practical tasks, will often take longer than you expect.
- Keep a record of previous projects and you will have some idea about how long things take.
- If you are getting hopelessly behind it is possible that you are trying to strive too hard for perfection!
- Ask your teacher or the technician for advice.
- Talk to students who have tackled the same or similar task before.

Here is another way of organizing a planning schedule:

This way you are regularly reminded how much (or how little) time you have left

WEEK	DATE	STAGE	PREPARATION	COMPLETION DATE	ACTUAL DATE COMPLETED	COMMENTS
20	26 Feb	Materials	Check availability	2 Feb		Start marking if time
19	2 Feb	Marking out		9 Feb		
18						
17						
16						
2						
1	23 Apr	Finish		30 Apr		

Fig. 5.25 Another planning schedule

The **week** column indicates the number of weeks left for the completion of the project. The **date** column indicates either the date of the last day of the school week or when you have your last CDT lesson in that week. The **stage** column may be repeated where that stage is to be spread over several weeks. In the **preparation** column you should indicate short-term plans, such as checking that equipment will be available. In the **completion date** column should be a date by which each stage is to be finished; the **actual date completed** column will be filled in when the stage has actually been completed. Alternative activities can be entered into the **comments** column.

Know what you have to do

Try to work out what you need to do well in advance. Arriving at a CDT lesson and saying to your teacher 'What shall I do today?' isn't likely to be very helpful. Your teacher will want to help but he or she does have to spend time with everyone and waiting your turn whilst someone else's problems are sorted out is not a very constructive use of your time. It's far better to have planned what you intend to do and if you need to consult your teacher before doing this it may only need to be to ask for permission to do something or use a particular piece of equipment.

Points to consider when selecting a project

- Is there a need for your project?
- Are you interested in the topic?
- Are you using previous experience?
- Will the project allow you to learn something new?
- Does your project fit coursework requirements?
- Have you checked the feasibility with your teacher/last year's candidates/other experts?

Hints for getting ideas

1 *Find ways to do things quicker*
2 *Look for ways to recycle materials*
3 *Be outrageous – silly ideas can sometimes become a reality*
4 *Apply new ways to do old things*
5 *Copy ideas but make changes*
6 *Combine ideas*
7 *Look for gaps in the market*
8 *Listen to people when they complain about something – you might be able to help*
9 *Find simpler ways of doing things*
10 *Help someone else*
11 *Look at the world around you*
12 *Watch television*
13 *Respond to design competitions*
14 *Try describing things by what they do*
15 *Read newspapers, magazines, comics, cereal packets, anything*
16 *Find different ways to do the same thing*
17 *Think about your hobbies*
18 *Go for a long walk*
19 *Write down all the things that went wrong today*
20 *Do something to help with other school subjects*

Whatever you think of, record your thoughts. You may not need the idea today, but tomorrow, when you do, you will have forgotten it! Use a chart something like this:

Keep all your ideas. You might be able to use them sometime

Subject	Date
Detail of idea	
Where did the idea come from?	
Possible uses of idea *Good points* *Bad points*	
Possible improvements	

Fig. 5.26 Record your ideas for the future

The design folio

Introduction

A design folio is evidence of the work you have done. As you work on a project you may keep the work you do and the information you gather loose but together in a pocket folder or separately. Before submitting for assessment you should gather together the work for each project into a folio or folder and present it in an attractive way. If you have magazine cuttings paste onto sheets of paper. Your folio does not need to be elaborate but should be neat and secure. It is not too important what size you choose but A3 has always proved a popular and suitable size. A4 is equally as acceptable. However, students taking the MEG examination should note that they do not allow the use of ring binders.

It is helpful for an assessor if your folio is divided into separate sections. As you read in an earlier chapter, credit is awarded under a number of headings and it will be easy for an assessor to identify what you have done and reward you accordingly if your work is well organized.

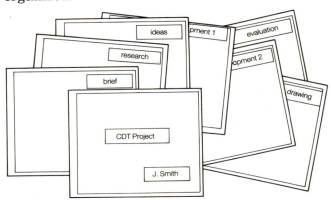

Fig. 6.1 Putting your design folio together

Each folio will need to be divided so as to identify the following sections:

1 Need or problem: you should say why you chose your project.

2 Analysis, research, investigation, brief and specification: explain what you did, present your findings clearly, state a brief and give a detailed specification.

3 Possible ideas/solutions: show a range of ideas which differ as widely as possible and show that you have thought about alternative ways of satisfying the specification and brief.

4 Development of the proposed idea/solution: give evidence for selecting your chosen idea and develop it as fully as possible. The idea may begin as a simple outline drawing and you should modify, perfect and change the idea until it is as good as possible.

5 Details of the final idea/solution: this should include presentation drawings and working drawings.

6 Evaluation: make sure you evaluate your work as you go along and that this is shown in your folder. After you have completed manufacture, test your project to see if it satisfies the need or problem. Make sure you report the results of your tests.

7 Planning: you must show how you organized the manufacture of your work. You can use a planning schedule or diary (as described in Section Five) or you can use a slip chart which is explained later in this section. Planning must show what you **planned** to do and what you actually **did** do. A record written after the project is manufactured is **not** what the examiner is expecting to see.

In addition, assessors will judge **how** you communicate your ideas. They will look for drawings in two and three dimensions, notes, graphs, charts, models and photographs. The assessor will also judge the presentation, organization and layout of the folio.

Up to 50 per cent of the coursework marks are awarded for your design folio and so it is worth making sure that it looks attractive and that it shows clearly **all** aspects of your work – sections 1 to 7 above. Be selective, an examiner looks for **quality** not quantity. Imagine how an examiner would feel if presented with 24 sides of A3 paper which only explained how the candidate decided on which nut and bolt to use!

Fig. 6.2 Examples of project folders

How long should a design folio be?

It is always difficult to give guidance on how much work to produce for a design folio but as a guide the SEG suggests that a reasonable folio will consist of a **minimum** of eight sides of A3 paper (they actually state a minimum of four sides of A2). Different examination groups award marks in slightly different proportions to each other. To summarize as far as the design folio is concerned these differences are as follows:

LEAG awards credit for all aspects of design work but does not break the activity down under specific headings.

MEG does not award marks specifically for 'planning' but all other aspects are credited.

NEA awards marks for all aspects of design activity with the majority of marks being awarded for making and planning.

SEG does not specifically give credit for planning.

WJEC awards credit for all aspects of design activity.

NISEC awards credit for all aspects of design activity.

Assessing the work of candidates

The following pages show the design work of a number of candidates. So that you can have a chance to assess it, the work is presented under a number of headings, corresponding to those frequently used by the examination groups. There is a description of what an examiner would be looking for with an indication of the grade levels candidates would achieve if the work was of the required standard. You should study the two examples in each section which are accompanied by examiner comments and then try to assess the third example yourself. Do not worry about marks, try to estimate the grade which the work is worth. Sometimes the third example will be of a standard in between the two previous ones but on other occasions it will be of a higher or lower standard. Only a sample of each candidate's work is shown (and please note that it has not been reproduced to scale): in a number of cases candidates will have produced many more sheets of work. Examiners do not judge work according to quantity, it is the quality which counts. Try to use your judgement to see how good an examiner you would be! After you have made your assessment you should look at the examiner comments that follow to see if you thought along the same lines as the examiner.

When assessing the work of candidates, examiners use their experience and written descriptions of what might be expected of a particular candidate for a particular grade. Appropriate descriptions are given before each pair of examples. They are **not** the descriptions used by any particular examination group but are shown here to give an indication of what examiners will expect.

Identifying a need or problem and writing a design brief

E grade: the candidate will have been given a lot of help. The brief will usually be written with no scope for wide interpretation. It will say things like 'I will make a box'.

C grade: some help may have been given but the brief will say clearly what has to be done. It will usually be expressed neatly.

A grade: the candidate will have identified a real need without assistance. It will state clearly the problem and say what the candidate intends to do about it. The brief will be printed, written or typed neatly.

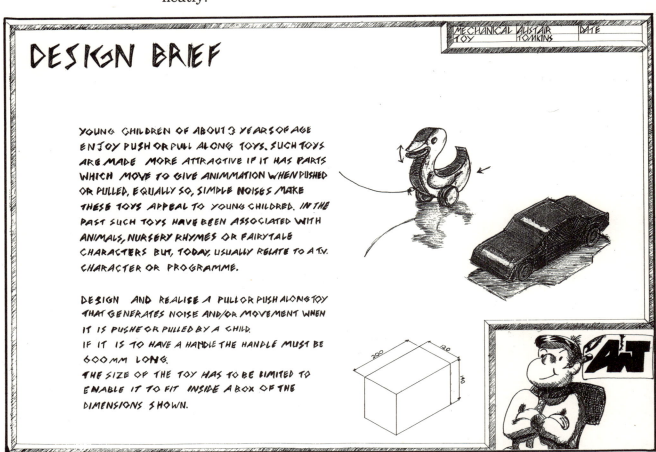

Fig. 6.3

Examiner comments

This problem is clearly shown and the design brief well expressed. This student has a very good idea what he intends to do. The drawings add interest. The logo in the bottom corner is a feature which this student carried through all projects thus giving them an individual touch.

Grade B/A

PROJECT BRIEF

The basic theme that I have decided to concentrate on for my project is that of fire safety in the home which after much investigation would enable me to design something which would help in fire safety. I considered investigating fire safety outside the home but I felt that this was not within my limitations and I also wanted to make a unique design and I felt this would be hard to do for most outdoor fire risks have been dealt with already. I wanted to investigate fire safety because it is a topic area which I find particulary interesting and I felt that if I could, in any way, design something which would aid in fire safety then I would be doing something useful and worthwhile. I also felt that there is room for improvement in fire safety because of the many thousands of needless deaths which result from dangers of fire. The aim of this project is to eventually after much investigation produce a design which would, in any way help in the prevention of danger through fire which could then be produced and implemented.

Fig. 6.4

Examiner comments

This project brief is quite comprehensive but should be expressed in fewer words. It says what the problem is and in a roundabout way describes the brief. It could have been more carefully presented.

Grade C

Now have a go at assessing this one yourself

Design Brief

I have a lot of fishing floats.
I want a wooden box or something to put them in.

Fig. 6.5

Analysing the problem, research and writing a specification

E grade: very little research will have been done and any specification will be vague and only include such things as how big? and materials. The specification will not show the limitations of the problem.

C grade: most of the important points will have been considered, but it is clear help from your teacher will be necessary. Research may be limited to cuttings from catalogues.

A grade: everything will be covered and very well presented with clear drawings and diagrams. Lots of research will have been done and the research will have been well presented in the folio. The specification will have been drawn up with reference to the research. There will be primary and secondary research. Photographs and drawings will be annotated.

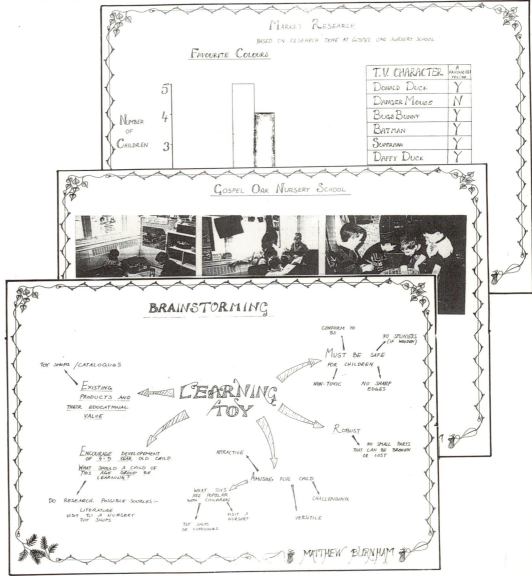

Fig. 6.6

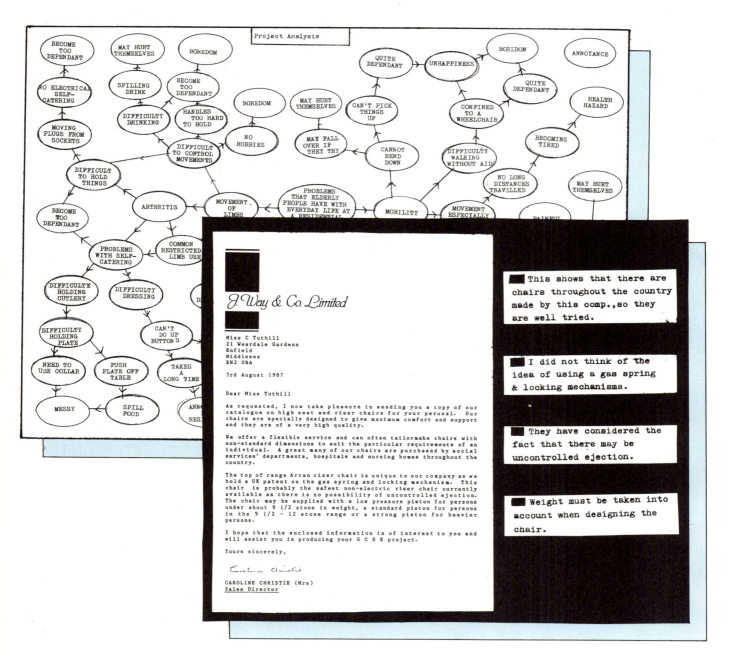

Fig. 6.7

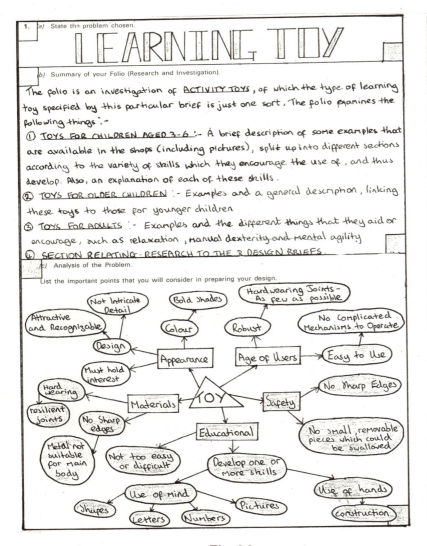

1. *a)* State the problem chosen.

LEARNING TOY

b) Summary of your Folio (Research and Investigation).

The folio is an investigation of ACTIVITY TOYS, of which the type of learning toy specified by this particular brief is just one sort. The folio examines the following things :-

① TOYS FOR CHILDREN AGED 3-6 :- A brief description of some examples that are available in the shops (including pictures), split up into different sections according to the variety of skills which they encourage the use of, and thus develop. Also, an explanation of each of these skills.

② TOYS FOR OLDER CHILDREN :- Examples and a general description, linking these toys to those for younger children

③ TOYS FOR ADULTS :- Examples and the different things that they aid or encourage, such as relaxation, manual dexterity and mental agility

④ SECTION RELATING RESEARCH TO THE 8 DESIGN BRIEFS

c) Analysis of the Problem.
List the important points that you will consider in preparing your design.

FURTHER ANALYSIS

① MATERIALS - Metal is not really suitable so the design should be made of wood or plastic of some sort. Wood is probably easier to use for the main part of the toy in most instances.

② EXAMPLES OF THE TYPES OF SKILLS WHICH COULD BE DEVELOPED BY THE TOY - Numeracy, basic sums, reading, recognition of letters, recognition of colours, pictures, tying shoe laces, basic construction skills, other manipulative skills, telling the time

③ WHERE THE TOY WOULD BE USED - It could either be used at home or in a playgroup.

④ BY WHOM THE TOY WOULD BE USED - It could be used to demonstrate things by teachers as well as children.

SPECIFICATION

① The toy should be made of wood or plastic, but not of metal. (Preferably wood in main body)

② The toy should not have any sharp edges or any small removable pieces which could be swallowed.

③ The toy should not be very big, otherwise it will not be able to be handled properly by a young child.

④ It should develop a skill of some sort, which should not be too simple or complicated.

⑤ It should be robust with few joints.

⑥ It should be stimulating & should hold interest.

Fig. 6.8

Ideas

E grade: there will probably be one or two ideas only. Where there are more they will be poorly drawn. The ideas will not usually fit the specification or brief. There will often be variations on a theme.

C grade: the ideas will match the specification but there may not be many of them and they may be fairly poorly drawn. Not much detail will be given.

A grade: Drawings (of which there will be several) will be clearly drawn. There will be a variety of solutions to the problem. Ideas will fit the requirements of the specification and brief.

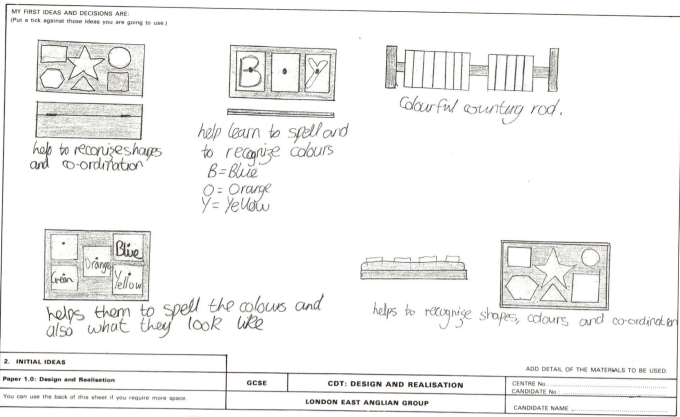

Fig. 6.9

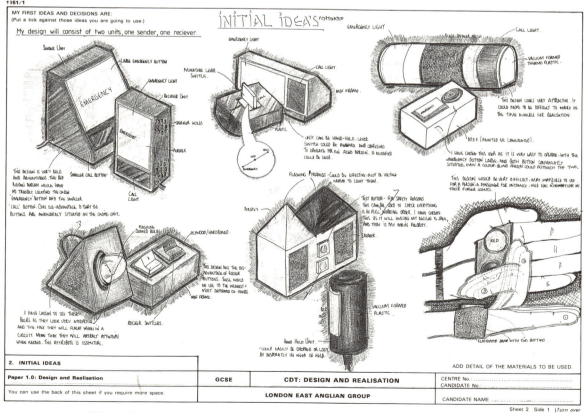

Fig. 6.10

Now have a go at assessing this one yourself

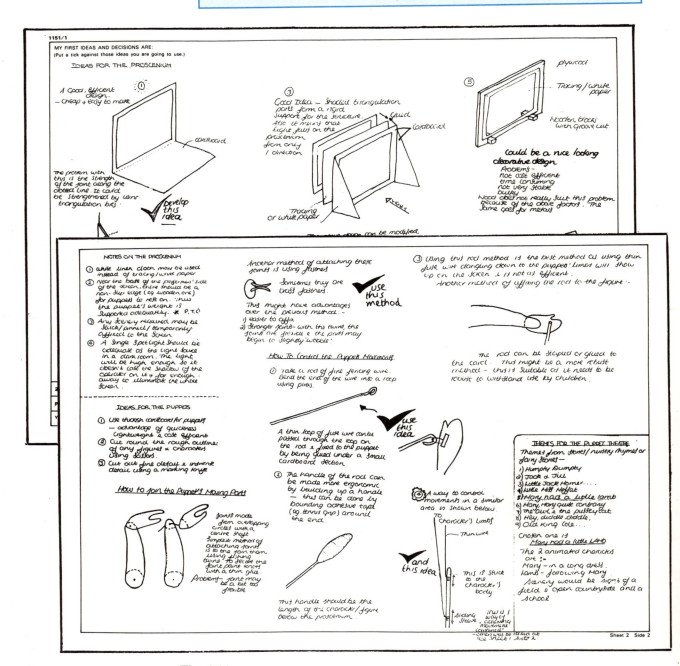

Fig. 6.11

Developing ideas

E grade: the original idea will not have been improved. It may have been redrawn. The drawings will be scruffy and few (if any) reasons will be given for choosing the idea. Colour and shading are unlikely to be included. Any colour is likely to be scruffy. Drawings will often be in two dimensions only.

C grade: drawing will not be of a high standard. The idea will have been chosen for at least one reason. The chosen idea will be developed through two or three drawings. Some measurements and details of materials will be given. Some colouring or shading will have been attempted but not usually to a high standard.

A grade: the good and poor points of ideas will have been considered. Many details will be shown. The drawings will be carefully done with colour and shading where it improves the drawing. There is likely to be a working drawing which will conform to British Standards. A pictorial drawing will be of a high standard. A list of parts is likely to be included. The development of the idea will be clearly shown.

Fig. 6.12

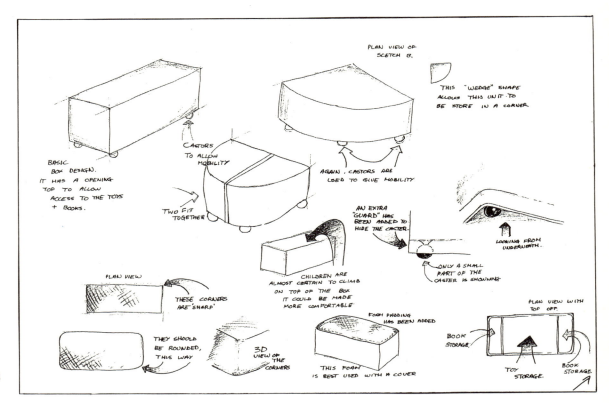

Fig. 6.13

Now have a go at assessing this one yourself

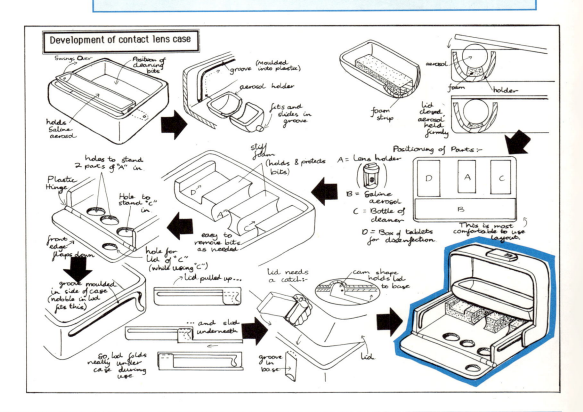

Fig. 6.14

Planning

E grade: there will probably be no written planning. Projects will not be finished and the standard of work will be poor.

C grade: the stages of making will be shown in the design folio and there will be some attempt to show what actually happened.

A grade: there will probably be a chart showing how the project was organized. The chart will show that the candidate has thought about the things which might go wrong and provided suggestions for alternative activities. The work will have been planned in a logical sequence. There will be evidence that changes to a planning schedule have been made where necessary.

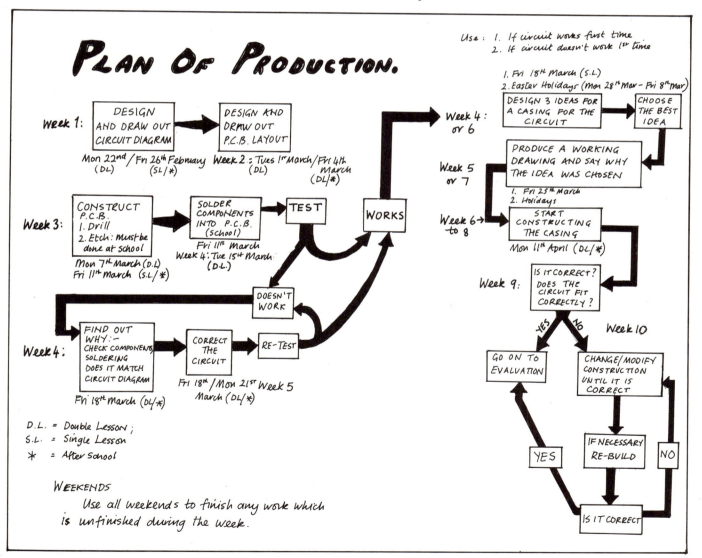

Fig. 6.15

Examiner comments

This student has shown most stages for the manufacture. Difficulties have been anticipated and weekends have been set aside for 'catching up'. There is no place to record what actually was done and it would have been easy to get behind. The ten weeks have not always been divided out correctly. Week ten, for example, would not be long enough for the whole of the evaluation process.

Grade C/B

By MATTHEW TUCK, 5 Dolbe

SPECIFICATION CONTINUED

b) DESIGN BRIEF

There should not be a switch which deactivates the alarm in case the attacker discovers it.

The alarm should be deactivated by removing the power supply.

The device should be as small and lightweight as possible.

The alarm should be as loud as possible.

Plan for Production   *Plan for Production.*

TIME PLAN

STAGES :-		estimate start	finish	actual start	finish							
SURVEY SITUATION	Bad weather unable to comp	5/6/87	7/6/87	9/6/87	10/6/87	CRITICISM	ADVANTAGES / DISADVANTAGES OF EACH SOLUTION.	7/9/87	28/9/87	30/8/87	10/9/87	
WRITE & AGREE BRIEF	DESIGN BRIEF AND SPECIFICATION.	15/6/87	17/6/87	10/6/87	12/6/87	FINAL DESIGN	DEVELOPMENT OF A 4th SOLUTION USING A PRESSURE PAD.	5/10/87	30/11/87	Casing not suitable need to design new casing.		
ANALYSE THE PROBLEM	PROBLEMS STEMMING FROM INITIAL PROBLEM.	22/6/87	30/6/87	15/6/87	5/7/87	COST	PRICE OF COMPONENTS AND MATERIALS.	7/12/87	9/12/87			
SEEK ADDITIONAL INFORMATION :		→	→	→	→	PLAN FOR MANUFACTURE	WORKING DRAWINGS.	13/12/87	21/12/87	15/1/88	18/4/88	
BOOKS / CATALOGUES	R.S. CATALOGUES, TANDY CATALOGUE	15/6/87	3/88	9/6/87	5/88	MANUFACTURE PART 1	ELECTRONICS Switch added	20/1/88	27/1/88	23/2/88	20/3/88	
LIBRARY	LOOKED UP BACK ISSUE OF "WHICH" MAGAZINE. NOV 85 FOR EXAMPLE.	THROUGHOUT PROJECT. Letters taken a long	THROUGHOUT PROJECT. time to arrive				2 PRESSURE PAD. Bracket has to made for switch.	3/2/88	17/2/88	10/4/88	12/4/88	
LETTER	SENT TO POLYCELL, TANDY, WOMENS AID. RAPE CRISIS CENTER, CONSUMER ADVICE.	1/6/87	7/11/87	1/6/87	8/8/87	3 FASTENING clips, not velcro needed to used CLIPS.		23/2/88	3/3/88	Velcro pads used.		
ASK PEOPLE	TEACHER, POLICE.	THROUGHOUT PROJECT.		THROUGHOUT PROJECT.		4 CASING (1) too not suitable big	Tools not available – next week	10/3/88	15/3/88	5/2/88	10/2/88	
EXPERIMENT	DIFFERENT WAYS OF ATTACK. TESTING PREVIOUS ALARMS.	7/87	7/87	7/87	7/87	CASING (2) VACUUM MOULDED. Must wait until machine is repaired		25/3/88	30/3/88	26/3/88	11/4/88	
OTHER	STUDY OF STATISTICS. FAULTS WITH PREVIOUS ALARMS.	7/87	7/87	7/87	8/87	ASSEMBLE	PUTTING ELECTRONICS INSIDE PRESSURE PAD.	15/4/88	20/4/88	Nuts and screws not available		
DESIGN 1	SOLUTION USING THERMISTOR.	29/6/87	10/7/87	30/6/87	4/7/87	TEST	SEE IF CIRCUIT WORKS AND IF PRESSURE PAD IS ADEQUATELY DESIGNED.	20/4/88	21/4/88	Running out of time		
2	SOLUTION USING MERCURY SWITCH THEORY.	20/7/87	27/7/87	8/7/87	20/7/87	EVALUATE	IMPROVEMENTS WHICH CAN BE MADE. Must get back on time schedule	21/4/88	21/4/88	30/3/88	28/4/88	
3	SOLUTION USING PRESSURE PAD.	16/8/87	31/8/87	5/8/87	17/8/87	MODIFY	MAKE IMPROVEMENTS. Modified construction	21/4/88	25/4/88	Doesn't work right, Think fault in thyristor		
						RE-TEST	TO SEE IF SOLUTION MEETS THE NEEDS OF THE PROBLEM AND WORKS WELL.	25/4/88	26/4/88			
FINAL EVALUATION	Time running out! Finished but not right!	22/4/88	30/4/88	30/3/88	28/4/88							

Fig. 6.16

Examiner comments

This planning schedule shows clearly that all parts of the project have been considered. It is evident that it has been used (handwritten comments and doodles). Because it is cramped it has been difficult to record all the work that was done adequately. It is, however, comprehensive and shows a depth of understanding and care.

Grade B

Now have a go at assessing this one yourself

PROCESS CHART

1 Investigation
2 Preliminary Sketches
3 Development
4 Working Drawing
5 Cutting List
6 Cut and shape two main arms of Design
7 Drill pivot hole into two main arms
8 Clean up the two main arms
9 Cut and shape the two supporting pieces of design
10 Drill pivot holes into the two supporting sections
11 Clean up the 2 supporting sections
12 Spray the four pieces of cleaned up mild steel bar
13 Rivet the pieces of mild steel bar together
14 Cut and shape the handle section
15 Rivet handle sections design
16 Sand and varnish
17 Write Evaluation
18 Hand in Nutcracker project

CDT PROJECT PLANNING

PRE-PLANNED WORK SCHEDULE (SLIP CHART) 1

Week	Work Scheduled	Slip	Work Completed	Check
1	Investigation		Investigation	
	Investigation		Investigation	
2	Preliminary Sketches		Preliminary Sketches	
	Preliminary Sketches		Preliminary Sketches	
3	Development		Development	
	Development		Development	
4	Working Drawing		Working Drawing	
	Working Drawings and Cutting list		Working Drawing and Cutting List	
5	Cut and shape the two main sections of the design		Cut mild steel bar to correct shape	
	Shape two main sections of design	Shaping two main sections of design		
6	Drill pivot holes into the two main arms	Shaping two main sections of design		
	Clean up two main arms	Shaping two main sections of design		
7	Clean up two main arms	Clean up two main arms	Shaping sections into main design	
	Cut and shape two supporting pces. of design	Clean up two main arms	Cleaned up two main arms	

PRE-PLANNED WORK SCHEDULE (SLIP CHART) 2

Week	Work Scheduled	Slip	Work Completed	Check
9	Clean up two supporting sections	Drill pivot holes into 2 supporting sections	Shaped 2 supporting Pieces of design	
	Clean up two supporting sections	Shape supporting pieces	Pivot holes have been drilled	
10	Spray the 4 pces of mild steel – sealing lacquer	Clean up the 2 supporting sections	Two supporting pieces shaped	
	Rivet pieces of mild steel bar together	Spray the four pieces of design	Cleaned up supporting Sections	
11	Cut and shape handle Sections	Rivet pieces of mild steel bar together	Sprayed design	
	Rivet handle sections onto Design	Cut and shape handle Sections	Design pivoted together	
12	Sand and varnish handles	Glue handle sections together	Hand sections cut and shaped	
	Evaluation	Glue drying	Handle sections glued together	
13	Hand in completed Project	Sand and varnish Handles	Sand & varnish handles	
		Evaluation	Evaluation	
14	Evaluation	Evaluation	Project handed in	

CDT PROJECT PLANNING   NAME _____ DAVID MANN _____   PROJECT _____ NUTCRACKER

Fig. 6.17

> **Examiner comments**
>
> This student has considered all aspects of the project. Work completed is shown and it has obviously been helpful in avoiding getting too far behind. Despite this the student seems to have handed in the project one and a half weeks late. It would be more usual for the columns 'slip' and 'work completed' to be filled in by hand and the way it has been done might imply that the whole thing was produced *after* the project was finished.
>
> *Grade A*

Evaluation

E grade: there will probably be no evaluation or if there is any it will be pretty pointless. Very few useful comments will have been made on drawings, e.g. 'It works because I made it well'.

C grade: evaluation will still be superficial. It will not be well presented and probably not refer to the specification and brief in any detail. There are not likely to be many recommendations for improvements.

A grade: there will be lots of factual information which will be well set out. There will be recommendations for future projects and drawings of possible improvements. Throughout the project there will be evidence of judgments being exercized and reasons for design decisions will have been given.

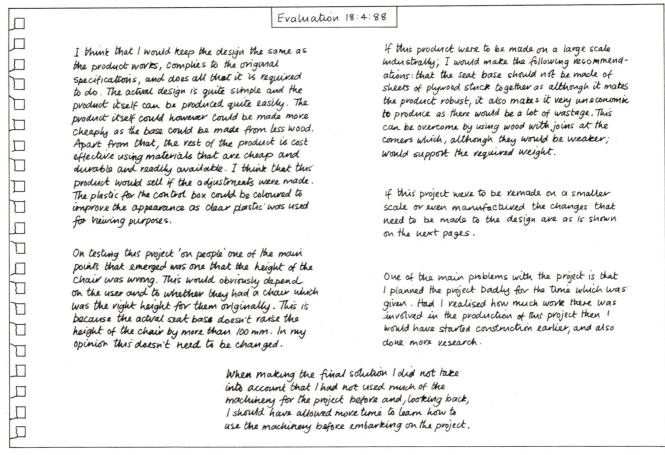

Evaluation 18:4:88

I think that I would keep the design the same as the product works, complies to the original specifications, and does all that it is required to do. The actual design is quite simple and the product itself can be produced quite easily. The product itself could however could be made more cheaply as the base could be made from less wood. Apart from that, the rest of the product is cost effective using materials that are cheap and durable and readily available. I think that this product would sell if the adjustments were made. The plastic for the control box could be coloured to improve the appearance as clear plastic was used for viewing purposes.

On testing this project 'on people' one of the main points that emerged was one that the height of the chair was wrong. This would obviously depend on the user and to whether they had a chair which was the right height for them originally. This is because the actual seat base doesn't raise the height of the chair by more than 100 mm. In my opinion this doesn't need to be changed.

If this product were to be made on a large scale industrially; I would make the following recommendations: that the seat base should not be made of sheets of plywood stuck together as although it makes the product robust, it also makes it very uneconomic to produce as there would be a lot of wastage. This can be overcome by using wood with joins at the corners which, although they would be weaker; would support the required weight.

If this project were to be remade on a smaller scale or even manufactured the changes that need to be made to the design are as is shown on the next pages.

One of the main problems with the project is that I planned the project badly for the time which was given. Had I realised how much work there was involved in the production of this project then I would have started construction earlier, and also done more research.

When making the final solution I did not take into account that I had not used much of the machinery for the project before and, looking back, I should have allowed more time to learn how to use the machinery before embarking on the project.

Fig. 6.18

Evaluation

Difficulties were found when trying to use the milling machine which was under much demand. The wood also tended to split when placed too high up in a clamp.

Time was wasted by not using the fastest approach to various objectives.

cont'd

Costs

Battery (Duracell for Long life)	– £ 0·56
Pine wood	– £ 0·15⁰
Rivets	– £ 0·04
L.E.D (1·5v)	– £ 0·05
Total	– £ 0·80
Suggested Retail Price	– 2·95

Fig. 6.19

Examiner comments

This evaluation is too brief and is restricted to comments about the difficulty of making. The absence of any comments about function suggest that the project may not have been finished. More credit would be gained if the student had suggested how time might have been saved. The costing is useful but ought to have been included earlier.

Grade E/D

Now have a go at assessing this one yourself

EVALUATION

There are both good and bad points to my project. Obviously, the fact that the final circuit which I built works as I wanted it to is a good point. The first circuit that I built also worked, but unfortunately, because the piezo was not loud enough, I had to modify the circuit. Initially I tested the modifications by connecting test leads to some components and soldering to some others. After quite a lot of testing, the circuit stopped working properly : instead of the buzzer (which I had connected to see if it was more effective than the piezo) giving out an intermittent sound, it just gave out a continuous buzz. Eventually I put this down to a damaged 555, as when it was tested, it didn't oscillate as it should have done.

One major design fault in the first circuit was that I forgot to include places for the thermistor connections, and if I had had to use this circuit, the thermistor would have to have been soldered to the underneath of the P.C.B., which would not have been very tidy. Another poor point of the first circuit was the soldering, which, although it didn't affect the working of the circuit, was not very neat.

It was because of this, and the fact that the buzzer (which I decided to use in place of the piezo) did not really fit on to the first circuit board, being bigger than the piezo, that I decided to build a new circuit.

However, the re-built circuit also has good and bad points. The soldering on this circuit is much neater than on the first one, but some of the components do not look straight when viewed from above - the wires on the resistor and the chips are not straight, due to the fact that I did not drill the holes for these in a very straight line.

Another bad point is that the circuit is much larger than I hoped, and than the first circuit - the first circuit was 84mm x 32mm, and the final one is 121mm x 41mm. There are reasons for this increase in size : one is that the buzzer is larger than the piezo, and another is that I had to change the size of the capacitor in the final circuit to one which is much larger, in order to get the correct oscillation that I wanted.

However, even with these facts, the circuit should not have been as big as it is. I could improve the size of the circuit and make it more compact, by leaving smaller gaps between components, and by putting the buzzer in a different place on the circuit board - over the preset in the top left corner, as it would just fit here, and the wires would reach from the position where they are soldered now. In all, I think I could reduce the size of the circuit to about 90mm x 40 mm (a reduction of about 30mm lengthways, i.e. 25%).

The Base.

At first, I was going to make a base with the battery and circuit board next to each other, but then I decided to put the battery underneath the board. This has improved the design, as it has made it much smaller and more compact than it would otherwise have been.

Unfortunately, the piece of wood which I used, although it was quite good quality, had already had some holes drilled in it - one which had to be filled, and the other, which was where the battery space is, was almost all taken away, but unfortunately there is still a small part of it left, which can be seen at the bottom of the space for the battery. This would obviously not be a problem if the base was manufactured.

The only other part of this base which looks slightly untidy is the battery space as it was difficult to cut out a hole neatly with the tools that I had at home.

The bolt which goes through the base to hold the case on was difficult to screw in. I did think of making a hole through the other side and then screwing it in easily, but decided to use pliers to twist in as far as possible, and then, by tightening the nut on the other end, pulling the bolt far enough through the hole to prevent the head fouling the battery. The bolt is there to hold the case securely on to the base and it does it's job well, but it does stick out a bit. However this will be at the bottom of the case, so is unlikely to be seen once on the wall unless it is positioned very high up on the wall.

The Mould.

The first mould made was not very good, as the edges and corners were not rounded very well, and it did not produce the correct sized case. The second mould was much better, although it was poor designing not to cut a large enough block for the mould in the first place. This made it necessary to stick on extra pieces of wood, as the block of wood from which the mould was cut was not large enough to cut another, larger mould. The fact that extra wood had to be added meant that all the cracks between them, which, if left, would affect the vacuum-forming process, had to be filled, which takes away some of the neatness of the block.

The worst part of the final design was the thermistor holder which fits on to the saucepan. The thermistor had to be coated with Araldite, in order to insulate it from the water, but this has not made it look very neat. However, it was better to coat it thickly, as I have done, rather than thinly, as then it might not have been properly insulated. A fault of the first design is that it is very crude, and did not fit on to the saucepan handle very well. The I shape was not very effective because the flaps were not quite long enough to fit over the thermistor and the metal was too thick to bend around the wires very well. This method is also time consuming as the shape must be cut with a coping saw and then filed down neatly, so I decided not to use this idea in my re-made design. The second design I have made for this part is an improved version, in which the clip would fold down around the handle, thus holding the piece in place. Another thing about the design is the piece of rubber on the end to protect people against burning themselves. This does the job but it is not on very securely, and with more time I would have tried to improve this part of the design.

The Case

The final case which I made was actually the third which was vacuum formed. The first two did not work well as the corners did not form very well. I think that this was because the mould was too high and thin for the machine to form a case around properly. A fault of the first design is that it is very crude, and did I made the mould higher than was needed to cover the base and circuit as extra height must be allowed as some is sanded off at the bottom to make it smooth afterwards.

On the third attempt, I cut part of the mould off from the bottom to see if I could form a better case. This improved the case, and is the final one which I made, although two of the corners still did not quite form properly and so had to be filed down as best as possible.

The final case is actually slightly too small due to the mould having to be cut down. However, the base can only just be seen from under the case so I left this as the final case.

Overall, the design does satisfy the specified need - it does sound a warning which is loud enough to attract people from all over the house, and it also fits the other constraints which I have listed in the specification : It is as light as possible but unfortunately as already stated it is not as small and therefore not as compact as it could have been due to the size of the circuit. If the circuit were to be cut down as stated, the design would be as small and compact as possible. Because the case with the circuit is to be put on the wall it means that it will not be affected by heat or water, and the only part of the design in water - the thermistor and metal are both resistant to it. The design is also fairly cheap as the cost sheet shows, and the plastic used can be cleaned easily. The whole design is also fairly strong - only the thermistor holder may be damaged as it could be bent, but this metal is quite strong and was used as it is quite easy to shape. A stronger metal, e.g. stainless steel would be less likely to be damaged but it is harder to shape due to this extra strength. Because I have made the circuit fit on to the wall rather than on to a saucepan handle, it means that it may also be used on some types of dish, but unfortunately, not all types. I could have tried to make the thermistor holder smaller so that it fitted on to dishes as well as saucepans.

The design can't really be used with mugs or kettles, although, again, if I had made the thermistor holder smaller, it might have fitted on to mugs and cups.

Thinking back, I don't really feel there was any need to consider making a product for use on kettles and coffee-pots as well as saucepans etc. as these are not as dangerous, unless the kettle is not electric; and most people nowadays use an electric kettle in their homes. The design also cannot be used in a microwave as the micro waves would probably damage the circuit. Making a design which work in a microwave would have made the project much more difficult so I decided against trying this.

The main way in which I could have improved the design is by making the circuit much smaller, but due to lack of time, I could not re-build a third circuit, as this would have meant building a new base and mould for vacuum-forming a case - a process which would have taken several weeks.

Even with the benefit of hindsight, I think one part of the design which I would keep is the battery being kept underneath the circuit board, as this would make the design very compact.

I feel that the materials chosen were the most suitable, and that the design would not have improved with a change in materials, except that, for mass-production, plastic might be more suitable for the base and the thermistor holder.

I also feel that the design could not have been made much more cheaply, and it could be fairly easily mass-produced in plastic.

The finish and appearance of the design would be improved by using a better piece of wood for the base, and neatening up the look of the components on the circuit board.

If these changes were made to improve the appearance and finish of the design, I feel that the design could well sell if it was generally available in the shops.

As it stands at the moment, my design is slightly unsafe to use, because the metal thermistor-holder is not insulated, due to lack of time, but once this is insulated, the design will be safe.

The design should last a long time, as, although the user will have to take the case off and unscrew the circuit to change the battery, the battery should last a long time so therefore it will not have to be changed very often.

One way to prevent the user having to take the design apart to change the battery is - instead of sticking the piece of plastic to the bottom of the base, I could design it so that this piece of plastic could be easily taken off, and the battery changed from underneath, rather than forcing people into the problems of removing the casing and the circuit before being able to replace the battery, and then of course having to replace the circuit and casing. However, as my design stands, this method could not be used as the base is screwed to the wall.

If the design is changed slightly though, so that instead of screwing the base to the wall, it is hooked on, then this method, of taking off the plastic to change the battery, could be used.

If I re-made the whole design from scratch, I feel I could have saved time by thinking more about each stage of production, as time was wasted by having to build two moulds and two circuits before coming up with the final product. Of course, if I had more time, I would have to build a third circuit, and I feel that, with more careful thinking from the start, I could have saved a great deal of time during the production stage of my project.

One final problem with this design is that if the battery runs down and does not have enough power to operate the circuit and the design is then used, the buzzer will not sound and so the liquid will still boil over if it is not watched.

To stop this from happening a device could be made which indicates when the battery is running out, and so unsafe to use, or the device could be screwed onto the wall with the screws going through one side, rather than the bottom. This leaves the base free to be made easily removeable, and so the battery could be checked whenever the user wanted. This would also save time and any problems involved with changing the battery as the device stands now i.e. with the user having to remove the whole case and circuit before getting to the battery.

Fig. 6.20

Examiner comments

This is a thorough evaluation covering most relevant matters. It could, however, have been improved by adding some illustrations of improvements. The features of this evaluation would have been easier to read if they were presented as a numbered list of points.

Grade B/A

Quality of communication

E grade: very little care will have been taken. There is unlikely to be any use of shading or colour. Drawings will mostly be in two dimensions. There will be little organization or care and a limited quantity of work.

C grade: some care will have been taken, drawings will be in two and three dimensions although three-dimensional drawings may lack precision. Work will be reasonably neatly presented. Ideas will be clearly expressed but will lack attention to detail.

A grade: there will have been meticulous care. Drawings will be precise. Charts and tables will be clearly shown. It is likely that more advanced techniques such as airbrush, computer graphics, shading, and highlighting will have been used. Working drawings will have been done according to BS PP7308. The work will show a range of techniques.

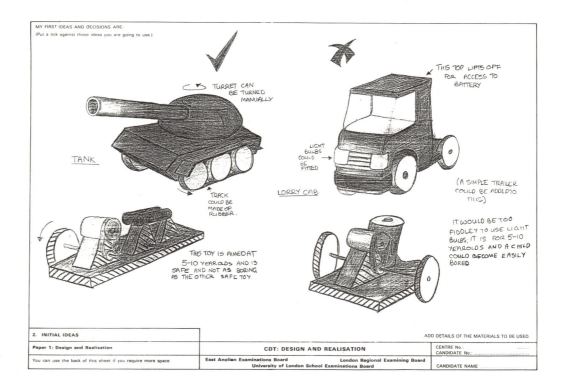

MY FIRST IDEAS AND DECISIONS ARE:
(Put a tick against those ideas you are going to use.)

✓

✗

TURRET CAN
BE TURNED
MANUALLY

TANK

TRACK
COULD BE
MADE OF
RUBBER.

THIS TOY IS AIMED AT
5-10 YEAROLDS AND IS
SAFE AND NOT AS BORING
AS THE OTHER SAFE TOY.

THIS TOP LIFTS OFF
FOR ACCESS TO
BATTERY

LIGHT
BULBS
COULD
BE
FITTED

LORRY CAB

(A SIMPLE TRAILER
COULD BE ADDED TO
THIS)

IT WOULD BE TOO
FIDDLEY TO USE LIGHT
BULBS; IT IS FOR 5-10
YEAROLDS AND A CHILD
COULD BECOME EASILY
BORED

2. INITIAL IDEAS		ADD DETAILS OF THE MATERIALS TO BE USED.	
Paper 1: Design and Realisation	CDT: DESIGN AND REALISATION	CENTRE No.: .... CANDIDATE No.:	
You can use the back of this sheet if you require more space.	East Anglian Examinations Board London Regional Examining Board University of London School Examinations Board	CANDIDATE NAME	

Fig. 6.21

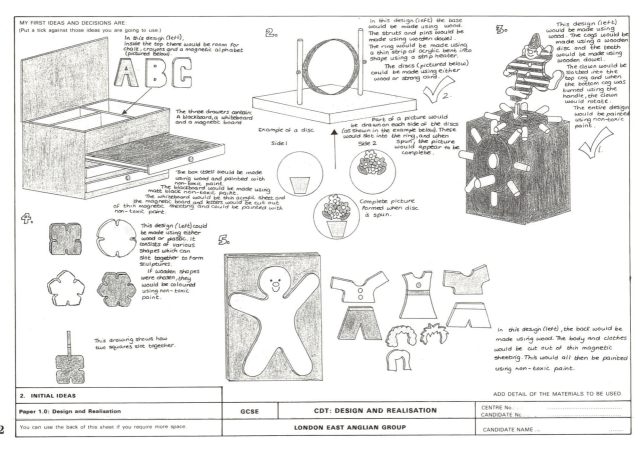

MY FIRST IDEAS AND DECISIONS ARE:
(Put a tick against those ideas you are going to use.)

In this design (left),
inside the top there would be room for
chalk, crayons and a magnetic alphabet
(pictured below)

ABC

The three drawers contain:
A blackboard, a whiteboard
and a magnetic board

The box itself would be made
using wood and painted with
non-toxic paint.
The blackboard would be made using
matt black non-toxic paint.
The whiteboard would be thin acrylic sheet and
the magnetic board and letters would be cut out
of thin magnetic sheeting and could be painted with
non-toxic paint.

2.

In this design (left) the base
would be made using wood.
The struts and pins would be
made using wooden dowel.
The ring would be made using
a thin strip of acrylic bent into
shape using a strip heater.

The discs (pictured below)
could be made using either
wood or strong card.

Example of a disc

Side 1   Side 2

Part of a picture would
be drawn on each side of the discs
(as shown in the example below). These
would slot into the ring, and when
spun, the picture
would appear to be
complete.

✓ 2.

Complete picture
formed when disc
is spun.

3.

This design (left)
would be made using
wood. The cogs would be
made using a wooden
disc and the teeth
would be made using
wooden dowel.

The clown would be
slotted into the
top cog and when
the bottom cog was
turned using the
handle, the clown
would rotate.

The entire design
would be painted
using non-toxic
paint.

✓ 1.

4.

This design (left) could
be made using either
wood or plastic. It
consists of various
shapes which can
slot together to form
sculptures.
If wooden shapes
were chosen, they
would be coloured
using non-toxic
paint.

This drawing shows how
two squares slot together.

5.

In this design (left), the back would be
made using wood. The body and clothes
would be cut out of thin magnetic
sheeting. This would all then be painted
using non-toxic paint.

2. INITIAL IDEAS			ADD DETAIL OF THE MATERIALS TO BE USED.	
Paper 1.0: Design and Realisation	GCSE	CDT: DESIGN AND REALISATION	CENTRE No.: .... CANDIDATE No.	
You can use the back of this sheet if you require more space.		LONDON EAST ANGLIAN GROUP	CANDIDATE NAME	

Fig. 6.22

Now have a go at assessing this one yourself

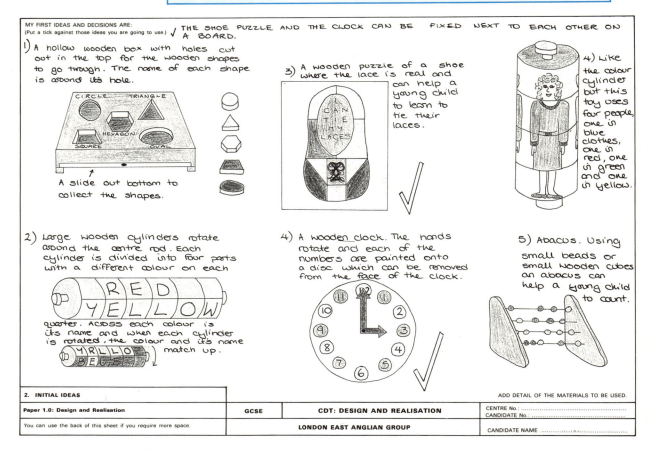

Fig. 6.23

Now try to assess your own work

Now that you have had a chance to assess the work of others try assessing your own work. You should have some idea of the standards expected. Try comparing your work with the examples shown on the previous pages.

- Are you doing better than you thought?
- Does your assessment agree with the assessment the teacher may give you?
- What can you do to improve your work?

CAUTIONARY NOTE

Getting a good grade for your folio is very important but you must also earn high marks for making your project. Don't spend too much time on one and neglect the other.

Making your project

Introduction

The purpose of this chapter is to help you produce good practical work and advise you how to best use your time. You will also learn what examiners are looking for and the standards they are expecting.

Don't forget the obvious

Designers often claim that making something complicated is easy, but producing a simple solution is difficult. How often have you heard it said that something is obvious when what was meant was it's simple! The fact is that simple is seldom obvious. You are bound to make simple mistakes which you don't notice and others will say are obvious, your teacher will, for a start.

Optical illusions

It's too easy to design things which are incapable of being made. This may sound ridiculous but it's true. Have a look at these examples.

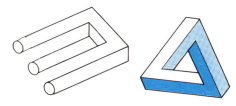

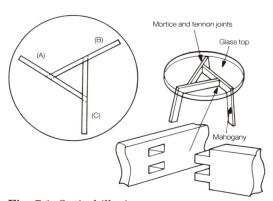

Fig. 7.1 Optical illusions

You will probably have seen some of them before. You may call them optical illusions and after a bit of thought you will realize that it would be impossible to make them. But what about the design for the table?

On the face of it, it seems perfectly alright. Each of the rails are mortised into the legs. That's fine, but the rails are mortised into each other and that's the problem. All the joints can be cut and fitted together individually but suppose you try to put it all together. (A) will fit into (C), (C) might fit into (B) but you'll never get (B) into part (A)!

> *Look at this example of a mechanical toy. Try to work out the order in which you would put it together*

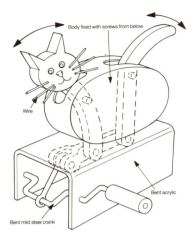

Fig. 7.2 Can this be put together?

It's obvious when you think about it! The steel crank simply cannot be put in position after the acrylic has been bent and the acrylic cannot be bent after the crank has been put in position. Too many students fall into the same trap as the sailing enthusiast who built a sailing dinghy in the spare bedroom and when it was finished couldn't get it out through the door!

Hint: *So remember: will it all fit together? Work out an order of assembly before you start to make it.*

Fact not fiction

> *What's wrong with this idea?*

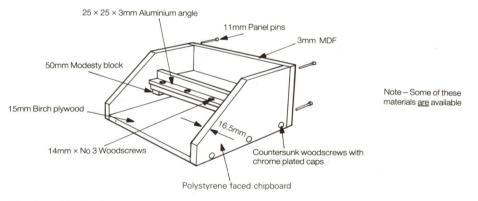

Fig. 7.3 Check the materials exist

It's not so easy to see what's wrong. Notice what the base is made from? When did you last see medium density fibreboard (MDF) 3mm thick? It's commonly available in 6mm, 12mm, 15mm and 18mm. There are other 'fictitious' materials. How many do you know?

Hint: *So make sure you are designing using readily available materials.*

Keep the cost down

> *Look at the illustration in Fig. 7.4. Can you suggest alternative materials which would be just as good and cheaper?*

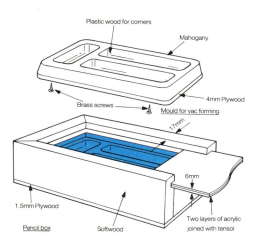

Fig. 7.4 Keep the cost down

The box is made from non-standard size timber. Use 12 or 15mm which is standard size and cheaper. 1.5mm plywood is too thin for the base. 4mm is suitable and in fact cheaper. The lid could be made from one piece of 6mm acrylic and save the cost of the glue. Better still use a single piece of 3mm acrylic. It will be strong enough.

The plywood used for the base of the mould could be changed for cheaper hardboard which would be equally good. Mahogany is far too expensive for the mould. Softwood or MDF could be used. Why are the pieces fixed with brass screws when gluing alone would do? Plastic wood filler is expensive, why not use polyfiller?

Hint: *Save money and natural materials by substituting other cheaper ones. Ask yourself 'Do I really need the properties of the material I have selected?'*

Record the changes

A common mistake made by students is to make changes (mostly to the dimensions) of a design and then not take all the changes into account when making their project. Examples of such changes are:

1 Realizing that a material is not available and substituting a different one.
2 Not specifying a standard size in the first place and then changing to a standard size later.
3 Increasing the thickness of a material to improve strength.
4 Decreasing the thickness of a material by substituting a different (stronger) one.

If you don't make changes to the working drawing it's all too easy to end up with things which are the wrong size, such as:

1 Boxes with interiors too small for the contents – because the thickness of the material was increased.
2 Units which are too big to fit into the available space – because the thickness was increased and the interior sizes remained the same.
3 Shelves which are too close together and hence too small for the books – because the thickness of the shelves was increased.
4 Lids and bases which have already been cut out ending up too small – because the thickness of the sides was increased and the box ended up larger.
5 Cylindrical parts being too small for the holes – because the hole was drilled before the cylinder (possibly dowel) was selected.
6 Joints not fitting – because one part (a mortice, for example) was cut with a standard sized tool (mortice chisel) and the other part (tennon) was marked out from the working drawing.

Hint: *Make your changes on the drawing as you go along and you are less likely to forget.*

Difficult processes

Frequently students are unaware of what can and cannot be done. It is not unusual for processes to be selected which are incapable of being performed. The following chart will remind you of some processes which should be avoided. There is space to add other processes as you discover them.

1 Glue gun is not a permanent method

2 Glue gun gels quickly, so warm surfaces

3 Some PVA glues stain wood and should be washed off before it sets

4 It is almost impossible to glue many plastics, especially nylon

5 Two part adhesives such as epoxy often set quickly, but still need thorough mixing to work properly

6 Wood glues such as PVA cannot be used for plastics and metals

7 _____

8 _____

9 _____

10 _____

Adhesives

1 Aluminium does not solder using most school equipment

2 Self-tapping screws shatter acrylic

3 Round nails split wood. Drill a pilot hole first

4 Wood screws do not hold well in end grain. Use a plastic (wall fixing) plug

5 Soft soldering large items cannot be done with a soldering iron. Use a bunsen burner or a blow lamp

6 It is dangerous to weld galvanized steel due to the production of poisonous fumes

7 _____

8 _____

9 _____

10 _____

Joining processes

DIFFICULT PROCESSES

1 You cannot drill holes in carbon or high speed steel (files or hacksaw blades)

2 Riveting needs access to at least one side for the pop rivet tool or a hammer

3 Through joints are stronger but need to be more accurate and hence take more skill and care

4 Acrylic requires some lubricant when sawing on an electric saw or it may weld itself back together

5 'Joints' cannot easily be cut in plywood and other manufactured boards

6 You are unlikely to have facilities to cast metals other than aluminium

7 _____

8 _____

9 _____

10 _____

Making processes

1 Oily and dirty surfaces cannot be painted

2 Gloss painting by brushes can be difficult. Consider using spray cans or dyes and varnish

3 Avoid scratches by sanding or using emery cloth in **one** direction only

4 Plastic dip coating is a good protection for steel but is difficult for large objects

5 The polishing buff can easily damage acrylic. Consider polishing by hand using liquid metal (or acrylic) polish

6 It takes a lot longer to remove scratches from the surface of plastics than to avoid making them in the first place. Cover surfaces with paper

7 _____

8 _____

9 _____

10 _____

Finishing processes

Fig. 7.5 Check if what you are proposing will be possible

Hints to avoid attempting the impossible
1 Check you can put it together logically. Draw up a list of steps or model it
2 Specify materials which are available. Is it a 'standard' form?
3 Keep the cost down by a sensible choice of materials together with suitable sizes to do the job

4 If you need to make changes to the design, change the drawing
5 Be sure that the materials you choose can be fixed together

Organizing your time

The benefits of organizing your time

Whenever you set out on a CDT project you are sure to have a limited amount of time available. There will be a deadline and your teacher will insist that the work is handed in on time. If you waste time you will not get everything finished and you are sure to gain fewer marks.

Some people always leave things until the last minute. Experience shows that if you do, you may end up rushing and then something is likely to go wrong. All of the subjects you are studying at school matter and careful planning of your time will enable you to do your best in every subject. Being organized can make you feel better about your work and the very act of planning your time will gain you credit in your CDT examination.

A suitable time plan

> *A student has planned the manufacturing of the project below. Can you see anything wrong with the way time is being used?*

> *This is the work of a candidate likely to be awarded a D or C grade in this part of the assessment . . .*

Planning sheet

Week no.	Activity
1	Get some materials out
2	Make parts
3	Glue together
4	Get other materials
5	Clean up with glasspaper
6	Paint
7	Test
8	Get fittings
9	Do an evaluation
10	Hand in

Fig. 7.6 A suitable time plan?

It is better to check at the beginning that all materials are available. This student has allowed only one week to make the parts and a whole week to glasspaper them. It is likely that the making of parts will take a lot longer than glasspapering. The student, therefore, has been unrealistic about how long many activities will take. A full week has been allowed for gluing up. This will only take an hour or so and might perhaps be done in the same week as the glasspapering. There are a number of operations out of order and enough time for painting has not been allowed. There will need to be more than one coat. The plan should also include a little 'slack' time in case things go wrong. A better (although not perfect) time plan might be as follows:

> *. . . and this candidate can expect one of the higher grades in this part of the assessment*

Planning sheet

Week no.	Activity planned	Work not completed
1	Check availability and fittings. Order special materials and fittings	
2	Get out materials	
3	Mark out parts	
4	Make parts	

cont'd

cont'd

Week no.	Activity planned	Work not completed
5	Make parts	
6	Make parts and fit together	
7	Clean up with glasspaper and apply primer and undercoat	
8	Paint top coat and attach fittings	
9	Test and evaluate	
10	Write evaluation in folio. Hand in	

Fig. 7.7 A better time plan

The arrows indicate that where work is incomplete it must be completed in the next week.

Planning ahead

When planning your work you will need to consider the following:

- The whole project and not just one part at a time.
- Arrange the operations in the best order.
- Have alternative things to do in case equipment or materials are not available.
- Allow time for things that may go wrong and need repeating.
- Some processes require to be left (paint drying, for example). Arrange to do it before the weekend or at the end of the day.
- Be realistic about how long tasks will take. If you've done them before then they will take about twice as long as you remember! If you haven't done that kind of thing before then it will probably take three times as long as you think.

Hints:
1 *Don't attempt the impossible*
2 *Things take longer than you first expect*
3 *Something always goes wrong when you've got the least time*
4 *Others can let you down*

How to get a good mark for making your project

Your teacher is the examiner when it comes to coursework and so is the one in the best position to judge how well you have worked. The marks awarded will be 'checked' by an assessor appointed by the examination group. The assessor's task is to ensure that your teacher is neither too generous nor too harsh when compared with other schools throughout the country. Many of the qualities which are assessed, such as how safely you have worked cannot possibly be judged by a visiting assessor and so the examination group will take your teacher's word for it. When the visiting assessors are judging practical work they will be looking to see how well it has been made. The assessor will have many years' experience and knows very well what constitutes a well-made project. The assessor will be asking the following questions:

- Has the candidate used appropriate materials and joined them together in a suitable way?
- Has the work been finished off correctly with edges smoothed and has trouble been taken with the parts which are hidden? Yes, the assessor might even look inside or underneath!

- Has a suitable 'finish' been applied or has it been plastered on simply as an afterthought?

- Does the project match the working drawing and do components fit each other properly?

- Does the product perform well and do what it was intended to do?

> *Try to assess the practical work shown below. Write your marks in the chart. To give you some help, most of Example 1 has been done for you. Some of the categories are very difficult to assess because you are only using photographs. The examiner, who has had the benefit of seeing the actual project, has already assessed these for you. Each category should be assessed out of 10 marks*

The photographs below are of:

1 A doll's house for young children.

2 A magazine rack for the sitting room of a modern house. It should display the magazines.

3 A rearrangeable sculpture.

4 A device to test if house plants need watering.

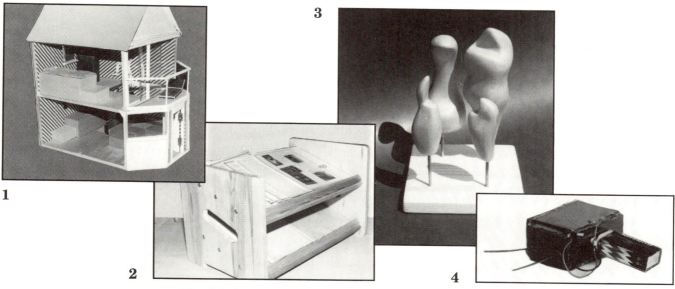

Fig. 7.8 Assessing the work of other candidates

Assessment category	Example 1	Example 2	Example 3	Example 4
Suitable techniques and materials	5			
Accuracy				
Quality of finish	5	7		
Does it function correctly?	6	6	10	6
Total				

Fig. 7.9 What marks would you give?

In the above example the marking scheme used is not from any particular examination group. It is given here to give you some opportunity to assess the work of others so that you might be in a better position to assess your own work.

Examiner comments: Example 1

The doll's house is reasonably well made but the choice of weak (thin) materials will mean that it can be easily broken. The colours are attractive and suitable and it is hoped the paint is non-toxic. The finish seems a little rough. Altogether it is a model which is probably better to look at than play with.　　　　*Marks: 20—25. Grade C*

Examiner comments: Example 2

A well-made project with appropriate choice of materials. If the shelves are made from 'solid' timber the screws may not hold very well. The applied finish is suitable although there is lack of care in shaping and cleaning the 'hole' at the side. It will not be possible to see the magazines on the bottom shelf without kneeling down.

Marks: 30—35. Grade B

Examiner comments: Example 3

An excellent piece of work. Well made and well finished. The base lacks a little sanding and might benefit from polish or varnish. It can be rearranged by rotating the parts and the change in reflection of light gives an interesting effect.　　　　*Marks: 35—40. Grade A*

Examiner comments: Example 4

The plastic material (acrylic) is quite suitable but the method of fixing (hot glue) is not. Putting the battery on the outside will mean it is easy to change but it makes the project look ugly. The project did not work electronically and the overall shape makes it unpleasant to hold. The angle of the 'probes' means they cannot go cleanly into the soil. All round not a good project.　　　　*Marks: 14—18. Grade D*

Displaying your work for assessment

Examination groups do not insist that you put on an exhibition of your work, but some do require the work to be available for a visiting assessor or moderator. If you can make sure that it is carefully displayed when it is presented for assessment (with the best on view) you will have the best chance that the assessor does not miss anything important.

Some pupils pile their work up on the table or bench, others produce a neat display either on a flat table or by pinning their best work onto a board or the wall. It will help the examiner and you if you take a bit of care.

Remember that the examiners will be rewarding your best work and so there is nothing to be gained by rushing and producing large amounts of poor quality work.

The following photographs show the same work displayed in two different ways.

Which display do you think shows the work to best advantage?

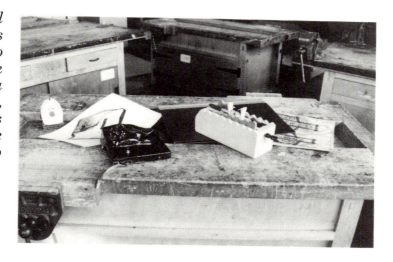

Fig. 7.10 Displaying your work for assessment

Candidates' work

On pages 86-7 are photographs of candidates' GCSE work assembled for assessment. Each photograph is accompanied by examiner comments and an indication of the grade which the candidate could hope to get if the candidate performed equally well in other parts of the examination. When assessing the work of candidates, examiners use their experience and written descriptions of what might be expected of a particular candidate for a particular grade. Appropriate descriptions are given below. Descriptions are given for all aspects of the practical work but it is difficult to assess safety unless you are the class teacher.

Grade descriptions for practical work

E grade

Constructional accuracy: there will be little agreement with the working drawing. Components will not fit properly. The work will not show much precision.

Constructional quality: there will be a low level of craftsmanship. Work will not be successfully completed. Some processes will be inappropriate to the materials. Parts will often not be assembled.

Quality of finish: minimum attention will have been paid to finishing. There will probably be no finish or if any it will not be appropriate. Parts will not be sanded, smoothed or cleaned.

Safety: there will be limited understanding of safety and the candidate will have needed much supervision.

C Grade

Constructional accuracy: the work will agree with most details of the working drawing. Dimensions will be accurate and parts will generally fit each other. Carte will have been taken in shaping components and there will be evidence that the correct tools have been used.

Constructional quality: a limited range of tools and materials will have been used, often a single material. The work will be largely complete and usually function as intended. Modifications will have been made and such modifications recorded on the working drawing.

Quality of finish: a reasonable finish, work cleaned and sanded. Applied finish will be appropriate but not always expertly applied. Some care will have been given to parts not normally seen.

Safety: there will be a good understanding. Close supervision is not needed for much of the time. The candidate shows a fairly high level of responsibility.

A grade

Constructional accuracy: all measurements conform to working drawing and agree with modifications. Components fit each other well. Machined components show a high level of precision.

Constructional quality: the most appropriate tools will have been selected. There will be a high level of precision. A careful choice of materials selected with due regard to cost. Materials will be carefully jointed with suitable and appropriate techniques.

Quality of finish: there will be a high level of sensitivity. Much care will have been taken during the manufacturing process to ensure no damage to parts. Appropriate choice of finish carefully applied. Care will have been taken with parts not normally seen.

Safety: the candidate will not normally have needed supervision. Checks will have been made before proceeding. The candidate is aware of the dangers associated with materials, processes and equipment.

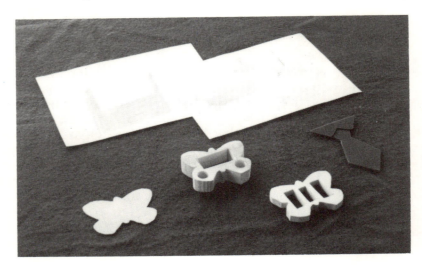

Fig. 7.11

> ### Examiner comments
>
> This work is not of a high standard. The design work does not show all of the design process. Work has been done in a range (two) of materials. Cutting out of the butterflies was not easy but it looks as though it may have been done with a band saw. The work is incomplete. There has been little attempt at applying a finish.
>
> *Grade D/E*

Fig. 7.12

Fig. 7.13

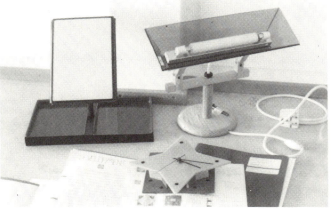

Fig. 7.14

Now that you have some idea of the standard which examiners expect, try assessing the two examples on this page. Do not worry about giving marks to the work. Try to assess the grade which you would expect the candidate to get. Compare the work with the examples given on the last two pages. Examiner comments and a summary of the grades which these two candidates might expect to get follow.

Candidate A

Note that there is very little design work

Fig. 7.15 Candidate A

Candidate B

Such a tiny piece of simple practical work to represent more than a year's achievement

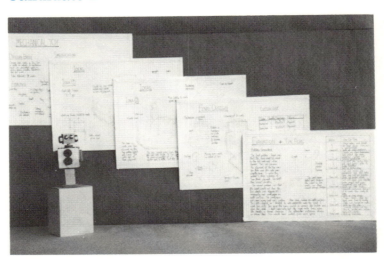

Fig. 7.16 Candidate B

Now try to assess your own work

Now that you have had a chance to assess the work of others try assessing your own work. You should have some idea of the standards expected. Try comparing your work with the examples shown on the previous pages.

- Are you doing better than you thought?
- Does your assessment agree with the assessment the teacher may give you?
- What can you do to improve your work?

Hints for good realization

1 *Quality is better than quantity*
2 *Check your design carefully before you begin manufacture*
3 *Plan a manufacturing procedure*
4 *Ensure that materials are available when you need them*
5 *Tasks usually take longer than you expect*
6 *Things go wrong when least convenient. Don't leave things to the last minute*
7 *You will be given credit for the good work you do. Marks are not deducted for what you do not do*

SECTION EIGHT

What do you understand?

Introduction

The following pages give you an opportunity to try out some of the skills which you have read about and which you will learn throughout your course. The process of design cannot easily be divided into convenient stages but for the purpose of this section you will be presented with a variety of tasks. Each task is concerned with one part of the design process. They are not linked together by a particular theme and success in one is not dependent upon success in a previous task. You may tackle them in any order.

How to tackle the tasks

Each task is presented on one side of the paper with possible responses on the reverse. You will learn most if you try them yourself before turning the page. Each sheet has a space for you to write or draw your response.

The amount of space provided will give you an idea of how much you should write or draw. There is also a time limit shown which will also help you decide how much detail to give. If you have difficulty with the first part of a task, leave it and go on to the next part. You can always go back to it later.

1 Identifying needs

This drawing shows some of the dangers in the kitchen.

On the chart below list some of the dangers which you can see and alongside write down some ideas for ways of preventing the danger causing injury to the young child. One is done for you. Try to identify six other dangers.

Danger	Possible solutions
1 The kettle can be pulled down by the young child	Design a hook mechanism which holds the lead near to the wall
2	
3	
4	
5	
6	
7	

Now think of six dangers to people other than young children.

1 _____

2 _____

3 _____

4 _____

5 _____

6 _____

Identifying needs: possible responses

Danger	Possible solutions
1 The kettle can be pulled down by the young child	Design a hook mechanism which holds the lead near to the wall
2 Saucepan can be knocked off.	Design a safety rail for cooker.
3 The electrical cable to the iron is worn.	Replace with a new one.
4 Cleaning chemicals are poisonous.	Design a lockable storage area.
5 Knife sticking out from surface.	Design a rack which encourages you to put them away.
6 Tablets (medicine) are loose.	Put in child proof containers and arrange to be out of reach of child.
7 The ironing board may be unstable.	Design a more stable one.

Hints:

1 Remember the young do not see danger and are always curious

2 Consider different types of danger: heat, sharp edges and corners, chemicals, heavy weights, etc

3 Solutions can either be products (artefacts), systems (ways of doing things) or changes in the environment (reorganization of the area, for example)

4 Now consider other possible projects suggested by the picture:
   a storage for iron before and after
   b easy ways of mopping up water
   c a way to avoid overloading the 13A socket
   d storage for the coffee mugs
   e display for the house plant
   f a safety device for the food blender
   g a washing up liquid dispenser
   h a better (safer) tin opener
   i improved handles for the drawers
   j better designed children's clothes
   k a device to prevent a saucepan from boiling over

5 Now suggest six more projects:

l _____

m _____

n _____

o _____

p _____

q _____

2 Identifying a need and writing a design brief

Time limit 15 mins

Have a look at this photograph of cleaning materials. The photograph was taken in a primary school.

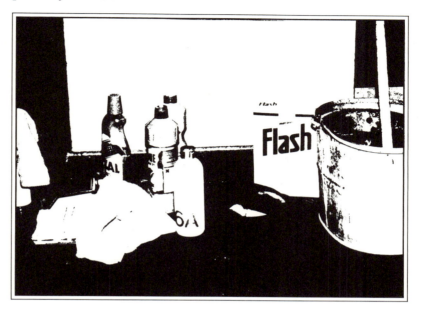

One of the needs which this photograph suggests is:

> Collectively all these items cannot be carried around very easily.
>
> Write a design brief for this need:

Design brief

It can be difficult _____

_____

_____

_____

Write down other needs suggested by the photograph:

1 Collectively all these items cannot be carried around very easily _____

2 _____

3 _____

4 _____

5 _____

Identifying a need and writing a design brief: possible responses

---

Design brief

It can be difficult *to carry all the cleaner's materials around the school. Design something to help.*

---

1 Collectively all these items cannot be carried around very easily

2 *Young children can be poisoned by cleaning materials*

3 *The mop might be difficult to wring out.*

4 *The items need to be stored upright and safely.*

5 *The cleaning containers may be difficult to open with wet hands.*

Hints:

1 *Do not let yourself get bogged down with one idea*

2 *Put yourself in the place of:*

    a *the cleaners*
    b *the pupils*
    c *the teachers*
    d *others*

3 *When looking for ideas for a container consider all the carry containers you know, for example:*

    a *kit bag or rucksack*
    b *cosmetics box*
    c *handbag*
    d *beer crate*
    e *shopping basket*
    f *supermarket trolley*

4 *Consider secondary problems:*

    a *can you accommodate a different make of floor cleaner?*
    b *if it might come in a different shape or size container?*
    c *if all items are placed in one carry container will an 'average' cleaner be able to carry it?*
    d *will all of the items be needed in the same place by the same cleaner?*
    e *think of other situations where a similar carry container might be used: at home, in the garage, at a guide or scout camp?*

3 Analysing problems and writing a specification

Time limit 20 mins

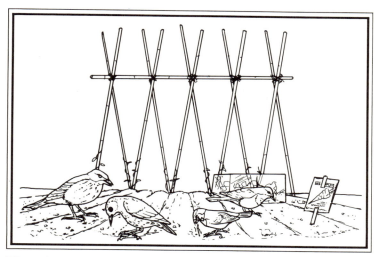

The picture shows birds having a feast on newly sown seeds. The area could be covered with netting but this might be expensive. You are required to design a cheap solution to this problem. It should take the form of a bird scarer.

What questions will you need to ask? Try to give some sensible answers.

Start by highlighting the key words in the brief. These may give you clues for the questions and then items for the specification.

Question	Answer
1 What kinds of birds eat the seeds?	_____
2 _____	_____
3 _____	_____
4 _____	_____
5 _____	_____

Now write a suitable specification:

Specification
1 The device will need to scare away birds
2
3
4
5
6

Analysing problems and writing a specification: possible responses

Question	Answer
1 What kinds of birds eat the seeds?	Blackbird, starlings, sparrows thrushes, jays, magpies
2 What kind of things scare birds?	Noise, movement, birds of prey
3 How much can I afford to spend?	Very little, Probably no more than a few pounds
4 Where can I see other examples?	Garden centres, farms, airports
5 Will noise of bird scarers disturb people in the area?	It depends upon the distance

Specification
1 The device will need to scare away birds
2 It should not look too unsightly
3 The cost should be kept as low as possible
4 It must be resistant to the weather
5 It must not spoil the environment
6 It should not disturb the neighbours

Hints:

*1 Highlighting **key words** helps focus on the important parts of the brief*

*2 Key words form the basis of the questions. The questions detail the things that need to be found out by either primary or secondary **research***

3 This need for research is endorsed by the specification

*4 The **specification** should consist of **short** statements – six will usually cover **all** the vital points*

Research and investigation

Time limit 20 mins

Three of you have been asked to design some storage boxes for a local primary school. You have decided to visit the school and research the problem further. You have already telephoned the headteacher and arranged a visit. You must now organize the research you will do whilst at the school. You obviously do not want to waste time whilst you are there and you want to avoid a second visit.

Situation and design brief

A primary school has been given several electronics kits. They are in cardboard boxes and the headteacher thinks the boxes are flimsy and will easily become damaged. You are to design a better storage system. Wooden boxes have been suggested.

List the tasks which your team will perform when you visit the primary school:

1 _____
2 _____
3 _____
4 _____
5 _____
6 _____
7 _____
8 _____

Working as a team of three students, show how you would organize the research for a one hour visit.

Student one	Student two	Student three

Tasks to be done on visit

1 Find out dimensions of kits, number of parts and sizes
2 Find out where kits will be stored
3 Find out which teachers and children will use the kits
4 Find out if all kits will be needed at the same time
5 Ask how much money can be spent
6 Look at and record dimensions of cupboards shelves, storage areas and de
7 Find out how soon the storage units will be needed
8 Observe the children using the kits

Student one	Student two	Student three
Interview with head teacher to discuss initial ideas Find out about money and time available	Talk to teachers and explain questionnaire Discuss difficulties with teachers Observe children	Investigate classroom: (a) space available (b) size of cupboards, shelves and desks Record measurements

Tasks to be done before the visit

1 Prepare a questionnaire for the teachers.
2 Gather together equipment which will be needed:
   a notebook
   b tape measure
   c tape recorder for interview
   d questionnaire
   e pencils
   f drawings of initial ideas to discuss with headteacher

Tasks to be done after the visit

1 Write down details from tape recording.
2 Meet together to discuss findings.
3 Agree upon future plan of action.

Hints:

1 This kind of research is very valuable but must be well planned in advance
2 You will get better and more useful information if you are businesslike
3 Other people's time is valuable. They will be more cooperative if you do not seem to be wasting their time

5 Generating ideas

Time limit 30 mins

When Mrs Greeves has to pick up the milk from the door step she has great difficulty picking up the bottle. She has asked you to provide a solution to help her.

1 The solution must be fairly cheap.

2 It must be simple to use.

3 There must be little additional risk of the milk being dropped.

4 It must use materials readily available in a school CDT department.

5 The device must be safe in use.

In the space below draw four ideas. Add notes to explain details.

Generating ideas: possible responses

When generating ideas try to ask yourself 'what really is the problem'.
It could be any of the following:

1 The lady cannot bend down.
2 The lady cannot lift the milk up.
3 The milk is too low down.
4 The lady cannot grasp the bottle.

Each problem can suggest a different kind of solution.
Here are four possible solutions. Notice how each answer approaches
the problem from a different point of view.

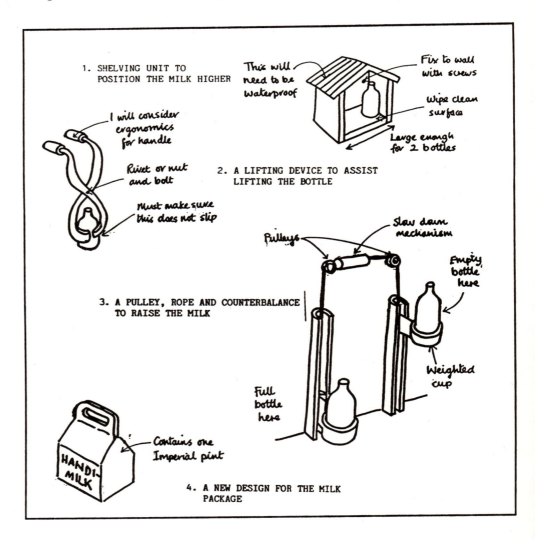

You may not have considered all of these ideas or you may have had
others.

Hints:

1 *Try to think about the problem from different points of view*
2 *Look for the weak and strong points in all your ideas*
3 *Do not worry if some of your initial ideas are a little 'silly'. After a
while even a silly idea can trigger off a good solution. When electricity
was first discovered it was thought of as no more than a scientific
curiosity with little practical use. How wrong you can be!*

6 Developing ideas

You have been asked to design a calendar for an executive's desk. It has been decided to incorporate a clock and desk tidy into the calendar. You have discovered a cheap source of quartz digital clock movements and incorporated that into your design. After putting down your ideas, you have decided that the idea shown below is best. You are pleased with the calendar part of the project but you are not yet happy with the desk tidy. **Develop this idea through four stages. Draw one stage of development in each of the four boxes.** You have decided that the design will be made from wood.

Initial idea

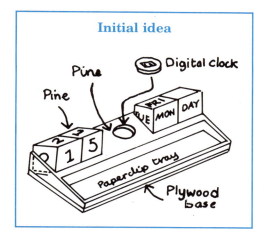

Development one

Development two

Development three

Development four

Developing ideas: possible responses

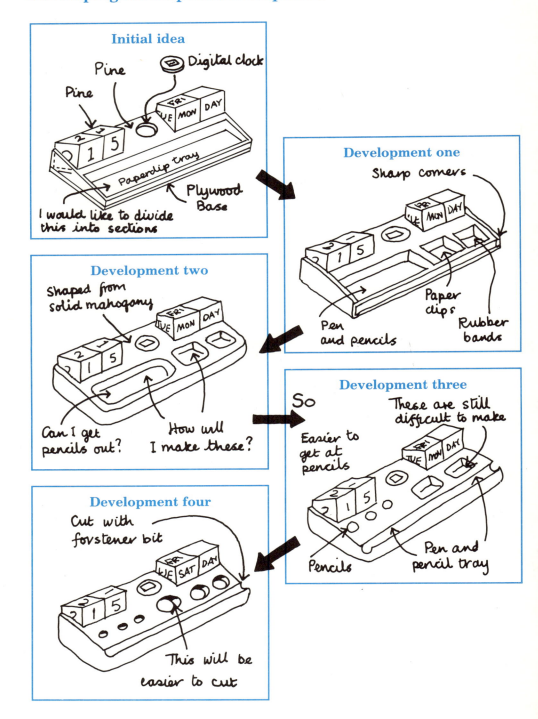

Initial idea

Pine

Pine

Digital clock

TUE MON DAY

2 1 5

Paperclip tray

Plywood Base

I would like to divide this into sections

Development one

Sharp corners

TUE MON DAY

2 1 5

Pen and pencils

Paper clips

Rubber bands

Development two

Shaped from solid mahogany

TUE MON DAY

2 1 5

Can I get pencils out?

How will I make these?

Development three

So

Easier to get at pencils

These are still difficult to make

TUE MON DAY

2 1 5

Pencils

Pen and pencil tray

Development four

Cut with forstener bit

TUE SAT DAY

2 1 5

This will be easier to cut

Hints:
1 *Try to make changes gradually*
2 *Change one thing at a time. That way you can easily compare with the previous idea and judge if it is an improvement*
3 *Give your thoughts/decisions on each development*
4 *At each stage consider the following:*
   a *can it be simpler?*
   b *am I using the best materials?*
   c *do I know how to make what I am proposing?*
   d *do I know how to join the parts together?*
   e *does it look as good as it could?*
   f *is it ergonomic?*

7 Selecting the best idea

John has found that during the last two months a fuse has blown twice during the evening. On both occasions he had to search around the house for the bits and pieces necessary to repair it. He decided to design a holder for all the bits. He began with this specification:

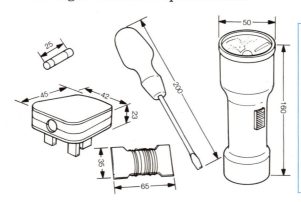

Specification

1 Must contain fuses/fuse wire, screwdriver, spare 13A plug and torch

2 Must be attached to the wall near to the fuse box

3 Contents must be easy to get at in the dark

4 Must look neat and tidy

John then drew the following three ideas. **Which** would you choose to make?

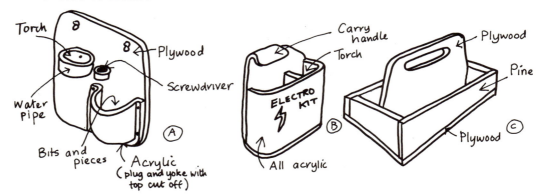

Check each idea against the items in the specification. Which idea will be easiest to make? Which idea will be cheapest? If you had to make it which could you make? Fill in the boxes with the letter of your chosen 'best' solution.

Contains all bits and pieces	
Able to be attached to the wall	
Allows easy access in dark	
Looks neat and tidy	
Easy to make	
Cheapest	
The one I could make	

Taking everything into account which do you think is the best solution?

Selecting the best idea: possible response

Different people have different opinions but consider the following as a reasonable response.

Contains all bits and pieces	C
Able to be attached to the wall	A
Allows easy access in dark	C
Looks neat and tidy	B
Easy to make	A
Cheapest	A
The one I could make	?

Now consider these points in more detail:

Contains all bits and pieces: all containers do contain all the bits but C is far too large and A might mean that the screwdriver would fall out.

Able to be attached to the wall: B and A could be attached but only A shows a specific method using 'keyholes'.

Allows easy access in dark: it is far better if you can get the torch out first. In solution B it would be difficult to get the torch out and in B and A the fuse and wire fuses would be at the bottom of the box.

Looks neat and tidy: this may be a matter of opinion but B does have pleasant proportions and the graphics are tidy.

Easy to make: A would be easy to make as a one off. C would take a little time and B would require some skill to form the acrylic accurately.

Cheapest: generally timber is cheaper than plastics but solution A is compact and uses less material.

The one I could make: this will depend upon you but consider what you are good at and what you have had experience doing before.

Which is the best solution taking everything into account?
Try giving each solution a score out of five for each heading.

	Solution A	Solution B	Solution C
Contains all bits and pieces	5	5	5
Able to be attached to the wall	5	4	0
Allows easy access in dark	3	2	3
Looks neat and tidy	4	5	3
Easy to make	5	2	3
Cheapest	5	2	3
Total	(27)	20	17

Best solution but I will need to improve the access to the bits and pieces compartment

Producing a working drawing

After having a number of ideas
for a jewellery box you have
decided on this idea. The
sketches are a bit rough and so
it is necessary to produce a
working drawing. In the space provided produce a drawing according to
British Standards giving as much information as necessary. Add a
cutting list.

Final idea

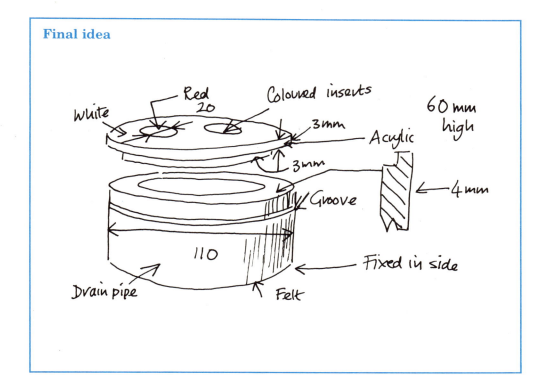

Working drawing

Has your drawing all the necessary information?

Producing a working drawing: possible response

This drawing is something like what is required. Note that all the main dimensions are included, but each is only shown once. Because this object is circular and hence symmetrical centre lines have been shown.

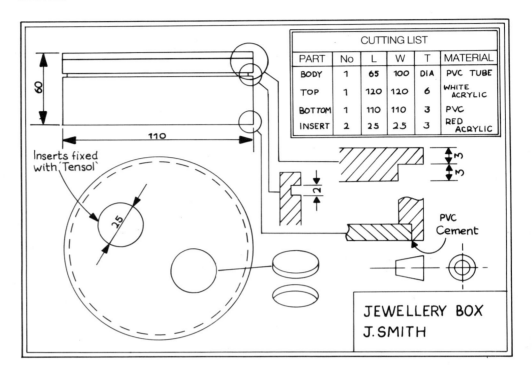

CUTTING LIST					
PART	No	L	W	T	MATERIAL
BODY	1	65	100	DIA	PVC TUBE
TOP	1	120	120	6	WHITE ACRYLIC
BOTTOM	1	110	110	3	PVC
INSERT	2	25	25	3	RED ACRYLIC

Inserts fixed with 'Tensol'

PVC Cement

JEWELLERY BOX
J. SMITH

You do not always have to produce an orthographic drawing to BS PP7308 and in those cases something like this would be suitable:

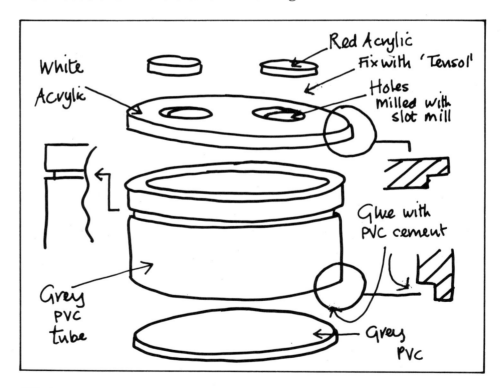

Red Acrylic
Fix with 'Tensol'

White Acrylic

Holes milled with slot mill

Glue with PVC cement

Grey PVC tube

Grey PVC

Hint:

Ask yourself this question —

'Could **someone else** *make my idea,* **exactly as I intend** *without* **any other information** *than that on* **my** *working drawing?'*

9 Organizing the manufacturing process

Here is a working drawing and cutting list for a young child's learning toy. You have five weeks to make, test and evaluate it. You have two one hour lessons each week and you are expected to spend one hour of homework time on your project. The toy will be varnished and the face of each block painted a different colour.

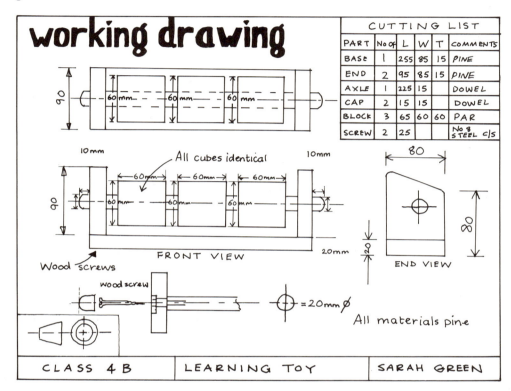

working drawing

CUTTING LIST					
PART	No of	L	W	T	COMMENTS
BASE	1	255	85	15	PINE
END	2	95	85	15	PINE
AXLE	1	225	15		DOWEL
CAP	2	15	15		DOWEL
BLOCK	3	65	60	60	PAR
SCREW	2	25			No 8 STEEL c/s

All cubes identical

FRONT VIEW

Wood screws

wood screw

= 20mm ∅

END VIEW

All materials pine

CLASS 4B	LEARNING TOY	SARAH GREEN

Plan a time schedule. Allow for things going wrong and don't forget that time will be needed for testing and evaluation.

Week no	Task	Description	Slippage
1			
2			
3			
4			
5			

Organizing the manufacturing process: possible response

Week no	Task	Description	Slippage
1 H/W	Select materials and mark out	Get materials out, check all available Mark out base ends and blocks Take home to complete marking	✔
2 H/W	Saw parts and shape	Saw parts and sand Drill holes Turn caps on lathe Sand parts at home	✔
3 H/W	Final shaping. Assembly	Cut axle to size and start cleaning Clean glue and screw ends Clean up	✔
4 H/W	Paint and varnish	Apply undercoat to blocks Top coat, varnish Rub down	✔
5 H/W	Details. Evaluation	Final coat of paint/varnish Test and write evaluation	

This is only one way of organizing the project. The important points to remember are:

1 Decide on a suitable order of tasks and estimate the time for each.

2 Write down the tasks in the 'task' column.

3 Make sure some 'free time' is left at the end in case things go wrong and you get behind.

4 Describe what you will actually **do** in the 'description' column.

5 Check **before** each lesson that you know what you intend to do and have an alternative activity just in case.

6 Remember the testing and evaluation and arrange to have a younger brother or sister or friend to be available.

Hints:

1 Plan your activities so that design and planning work not needing specialist equipment is done at home
2 Arrange for glue and paint, etc, to be allowed to dry over a weekend or holiday
3 Homework time may be time spent at school but make sure it is not in lesson time, e.g. lunchtimes
4 Remember that planning ahead not only saves time but is likely to get you higher marks

10 Evaluating solutions

A pupil has produced this solution to a design problem.

Here is the design brief to which the pupil worked.

> **Design brief**
>
> I can see a lot of birds from the balcony of our flat. I will design a bird table and nesting box to attract them

	HOW I PLANNED MY TIME	
WEEK	TASK	SLIPPAGE
1	Get materials	Some materials missing
2	Mark out	Only just started
3	Cut to shape	Cut top only
4	Finish shaping	Cut rest of pieces
5	Drill holes Sand	Drilled wrong holes, must make pieces again
6	Assemble	Still some parts to make
7	Varnish	Assemble next week
8	Evaluate	Won't varnish-don't want it pretty!

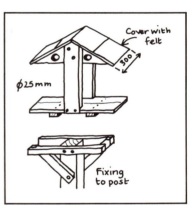

Take a careful look at the finished product and try to decide how well it satisfies the brief. Compare it with the working drawing. Do you think the time was well organized? As far as you can write an evaluation of the finished product. Use the following headings:

Does the solution satisfy the brief?

_____

_____

_____

_____

Were there any obvious problems with the manufacture?

_____

_____

_____

_____

Can you give any recommendations for improvements or changes in the manufacturing procedure?

_____

_____

_____

_____

Evaluating solutions: possible response

Does the solution satisfy the brief?

It is impossible to say if the product works as a bird nesting box but the 'table' seems large enough. Had the project been better researched it would have been discovered that a nesting/feeding unit does not normally work. Birds will **not** nest due to overpopulation of the table at feeding times. The solution has all of the requirements to attract birds: table, nesting box, perches. Above the ground the birds will be protected from cats. It is unlikely to meet the requirements of the brief if it is intended for a balcony. The post cannot be driven into the ground. It might be better to consider fixing to the wall next time.

Were there any obvious problems with the manufacture?

The finished product looks like the working drawing but differs in a few details (addition of perches and slight enlargement of the nesting box and access holes). The planning schedule shows that time was well allocated to the different tasks but a problem arose with fixing the box to the post. Holes for the perches were drilled too large and this meant the uprights had to be replaced. Having lost time, there was little chance to catch up and so the product might have been rushed at the end. More time should have been allowed for making and a little free time might have been left in case things went wrong.

Can you give any recommendations for improvements or changes in the manufacturing procedure?

If the working drawing had been changed when the design was altered materials may not have been wasted. More research might have meant that the table would have been better. The nesting area is quite large and might be better if it were smaller. It was a serious oversight to make the solution with a post which needed to be fixed into the ground. Even a post with a stand might take up too much room on the balcony. A design where the box and table hung from the edge of the balcony could be considered; it would not take up balcony space and the birds would not need to come too close to the flat. This would encourage them. There would also be less mess on the balcony. It was a mistake not to varnish to box. Varnishing not only improves the appearance but protects the timber from the weather. A preservative, such as creosote, would protect the timber better, but might be toxic.

Hints:

1 *In a full evaluation you would also compare the design with the details of the specification*
2 *You would also test the design. You might, for example, mount the nesting box/table on the balcony and over a month or so record which types of bird were attracted to it*
3 *Over a longer period you could see which types of bird took up residence in the nesting box*
4 *If you had wanted to restrict the box to smaller birds such as tits the access hole can be very small*
5 *It is possible that mice might be attracted to the nesting box!*

Doing well in written examinations

Introduction

Broadly speaking, all CDT:Design and Realization syllabuses aim at assessing the same things and have a similar content. Some examination groups may emphasize one area or another and others may leave some details out (SEG, for example, asks simple technological questions requiring calculations, and MEG have tended to ignore environmental issues). However, all examination groups will expect you to have a working understanding of the topics outlined in this chapter. Do bear in mind, however, that this chapter is not fully comprehensive and more details can be found in any good CDT theory book.

It is **very important** to realize that the topics outlined in this section cannot be treated separately and that you are unlikely to be asked to simply recall knowledge, e.g. you will not be asked to produce labelled diagrams of tools or provide a list of the properties of mild steel.

Although some short answer questions will often be restricted to information and understanding from one area only, longer answer questions will not. Questions are set which test your ability to apply your knowledge and understanding to situations, such as choosing a material for a particular purpose where there could easily be more than one suitable answer. At the end of this chapter there are a number of short answer questions and examples of longer answer questions which aim to test a wider understanding of CDT. All of the specimen questions have been taken from GCSE examination papers.

What you are expected to know and understand

The following headings suggest areas where you can concentrate your revision. Most of your learning takes place whilst you are undertaking your 'design and make' projects. The two sections, Design and Technology in Society, and Technology – the application of human knowledge are sometimes not covered in school in quite as much detail as other sections and so you would be wise to spend a little extra time revising these topics.

Materials

During your course you will have learned a great deal about designing and making and you will have had a lot of experience of using materials. The following section will remind you of the materials which you may have used. You are not expected to be fully familiar with all of them.

What materials should you know about?

For example, timber, metals, plastics, ceramics, textiles, concrete, paper products, and so on.

Timber

Hardwoods

Do you know about these specific hardwoods?

Material	Use
Mahogany	Furniture
Beech	Kitchenware
Oak	Church beams
Teak	Garden seats
Balsa	Aircraft models

Softwoods

You are unlikely to have used all of these specific (named) softwoods.

Material	Use
Scots Pine	General joinery
Spruce	Packing cases
Douglas Fir	Ladders
Red Cedar	Garden fencing
Parana Pine	Quality joinery

Manufactured boards

They are a good way of improving on the properties of natural timber.

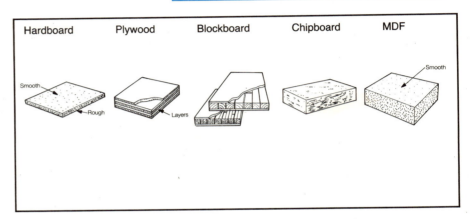

Metals

Ferrous metals

They contain iron (and so rust) and are usually magnetic.

Material	Use
Cast iron	Engineer's vice
Mild steel	Nails, car bodies
Carbon steel	Chisels, saws
Wrought iron	Decorative garden gates

Non-ferrous metals

They do not contain iron.

Material	Use
Aluminium	Saucepans
Copper	Electric wires
Tin	Coating steel
Zinc	Torch batteries
Lead	Car batteries

Alloys

They are mixtures of two or more metals.

Material	Use
Durallumin	Aircraft parts
Brass (Cu/Zn)	Letterboxes
Bronze (Cu/Sn)	Bearings
Stainless steel	Cutlery
High speed steel	Lathe tools

Plastics

Thermoplastics

They all soften with heat and hence can be reformed by heating. They are often flexible and are excellent electrical insulators.

Material	Use
Acrylic	Plastic baths
PVC	Gutters
Polystyrene	Model kits
Polythene	Mixing bowls
Nylon	Combs

Thermosetting plastics

In manufacture heat causes them to harden and hence they cannot be reformed.

Material	Use
Polyester	GRP, castings
Urea formaldehyde	Electrical fittings
Epoxy	Araldite
Melamine	Worktops

Availability of materials

Know about stock sizes and forms of supply.

You can't get metals in the same sizes as timber.

Timber	Metal	Plastics
Planks	Strip	Sheet
Sheets	Rod	Rod
Boards	Sheet	Foam
Squares	Tube	Liquid
Dowel	Angle	Granules

Costs of materials

The costs of materials vary and you should always consider this in your designs.

Is there a cheaper material which will do the job equally well?

Cost Increasing →

Gold, Silver, Platinum
Copper, Brass, Lead
Aluminium, Acrylic, Hardwood
Blockboard, Softwood, Plywood
Hardboard, Chipboard
Cardboard, Paper

Properties of materials

Hardness
Resistance to scratching: balsa = soft, mild steel = hard.
Stiffness
Resistance to distortion: wrought iron = malleable, copper = ductile.
Strength
Tension, compression, bending, twisting, shearing (there are further details on page 120)
Electrical resistance
How easily will a current flow through it?
Thermal properties
Will it conduct heat or is it a good insulator?
Appearance
What colour is it? Is it transparent or opaque?
Texture
How does it feel to touch?
Resistance to corrosion
Does it rust or is it affected by the weather, acids, alkalis, sea water, etc?
Working properties
How do you shape the material? Is heat needed? Can it be machined and do you know how? Are there any special precautions you should adopt, such as to prevent breathing in dust? Will it accept fixings such as nails or screws? What kind of finish should be used?

Selecting the best materials

Sizes and forms
What standard sizes and forms are manufactured?

Availability
Is it in stock?

Cost
Is there a cheaper alternative?

Properties
What is required?

> *It's really a compromise between all four*

113

Making things

Processes

There are four main ways of converting raw materials into shaped products:

Fabricating
Assembling a number of parts.

Joints, welding, brazing, soldering, nails, screws, pop rivets, knockdown fittings, adhesives.

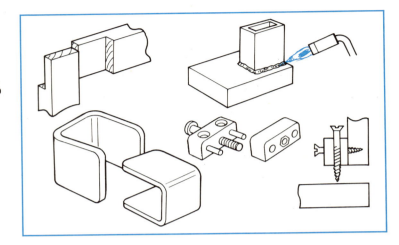

Deforming
Rearranging the shape or form of a material.

Forging, hollowing, bending, acrylic forming, vacuum forming, etc.

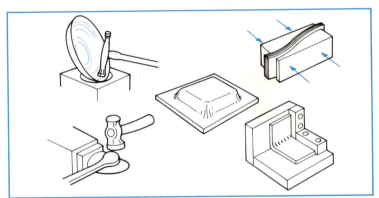

Wasting
Cutting away unwanted material.

Machining, cutting joints, drilling holes.

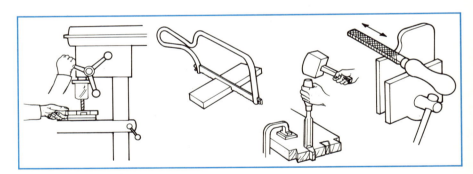

Casting and moulding
Pouring or forcing a liquid or softened material into a mould or die.

Aluminium casting, injection moulding, blow moulding.

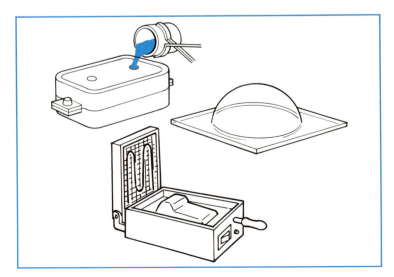

Organizing the manufacturing process

What is automation?

Automatic machines and robots are expensive but can produce products at lower cost.

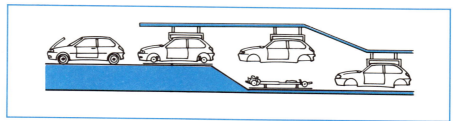

What are mass produced products?
Are there advantages?

What is batch production?
How big is a batch?

Mass	Batch	One-off
Pencils	Books	Racing car
Cars	Newspapers	CDT project
Cassette tapes	TV sets	Space shuttle

Can you give examples of 'one-off' production?

Flow charts

Can you produce a flow chart to show how you would organize a manufacturing process?

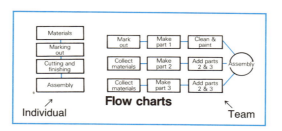

Assembly principles

Use the correct process

Make sure the parts can be fixed together (e.g. you cannot solder aluminium easily).

Get the order correct

Organize the order in which parts will be assembled. Do not try to do all the assembly in one go.

Don't be in a hurry

Remember, some processes take time, e.g. glue, soldering.

> **Correct processes?**
> **Correct order?**
> **Leave to set or cool?**

Finishing things off

Reasons
Corrosion resistance, appearance, protection, wear, lubrication.

Layer finishes
Paint, varnish, coatings, plating.

Surface modification
Textures, knurling.

Penetrative finishes
Creosote, case hardening for steel.

Abrasives
Glasspaper, wire wool, emery cloth, water of ayr stone.

Finish	Use
Varnish	Sealing, shine
Paint	Protecting, colour
Textured paint	Non-slip
Knurling	Grip
Galvanizing	Prevent rusting
Chrome plate	Shine
Case hardening	Reduce wear
Creosote	Prevent rotting
Glasspaper	Smooth timber
Emery cloth	Smooth metals
Water of ayr stone	High polish for metal
Dip coating	Plastic coating

Hand tools

Rule, gauges, squares.

Careful marking out means your parts are more likely to fit.

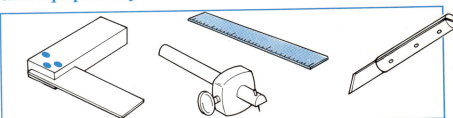

Saws, shears, knives, planes, etc.

Try to use the best one for the purpose. They are used to change the shape, size and form of a material. Most of these cutting tools use a wedge action to perform the cutting.

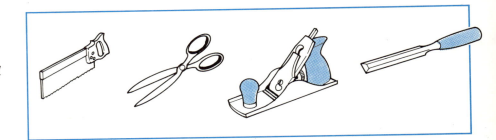

Cramps, vice, pliers, etc.

Keep it held securely and in the best position to be worked on.

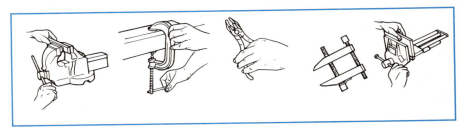

Drills, braces, bits, holesaw, conecut, bradawl.

Different materials and different size holes need different tools.

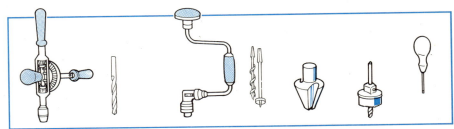

Screwdrivers, spanners, pincers, pop rivet tool.

These tools are used to assist with securing and removing fixings such as screws and nuts and bolts.

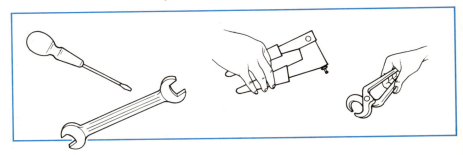

Hammers and mallets.

Used to strike materials and tools. Do not hit tools with a metal hammer if it might damage them. Soft hammers (copper or plastic faced) can be used to avoid damage.

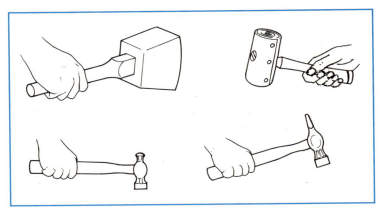

Machine tools

Pillar drill, lathes, milling machine, sanders, band saw.

Remember what they are used for and be particularly careful about following safety precautions.

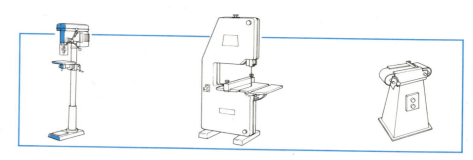

Hand-held power tools, drill, orbital sander, jig saw.

These speed up the work but take care—they often require more skill than hand tools.

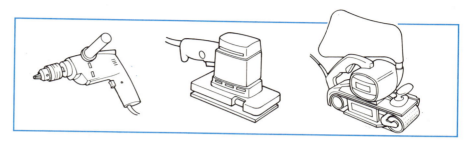

Plastics forming equipment

Vacuum former, strip heater, injection moulding machine, fluidizing tank

Heat is always needed.

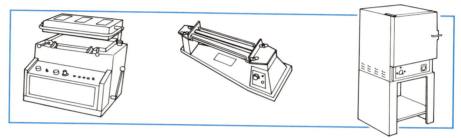

Safety is very important

Throughout the whole of your CDT course you are expected to concern yourself with safety and safe working practices. The following list will help you to concentrate your effort.

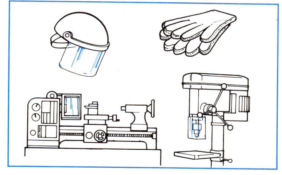

Safety in design

Sharp edges and corners, moving parts, electricity, surface finish, strength. Correct materials and construction. Safe structures.

Avoid injury to people.

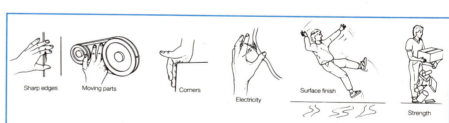

Safety in the home

Children, the elderly, bathrooms, cooking, the garage.

Safety in the CDT department

Safety equipment, personal equipment, emergencies, first aid, safe use of tools and machines.

Know and apply safety rules and know what to do in an emergency. Where are the fire extinguishers kept? Do you know how to use them?

SAFETY CODE
1 Wear goggles and other safety equipment
2 Tie long hair back and tuck in ties
3 Hold work securely
4 Know what to do in an emergency
5 Never work alone in the workshop
6 Follow your teacher's instructions

Electrical safety

Mains equipment, earthing and fuses. Action after an accident.

Can you wire a 13 amp plug? What is the function of earthing? What is the function of an RCCB?

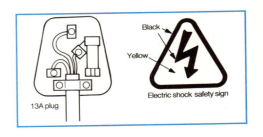

13A plug

Black

Yellow

Electric shock safety sign

Designing – satisfying needs and solving problems

1 Human needs

Protection, warmth, comfort, entertainment, employment, food and drink.

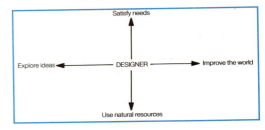

Satisfy needs

Explore ideas ← DESIGNER → Improve the world

Use natural resources

2 Consider the needs of specialist groups

a Doctors, engineers, sailors, etc.
b Disability – physical, mental, sight, hearing.
c Children – sizes, experience, learning, entertainment.
d The elderly – what are their particular needs?

3 Ergonomics/anthropometrics

a Human attributes and limitations.
b Use of mock-ups and an ergonome.

4 Environmental needs
Protection, conservation, improvement.

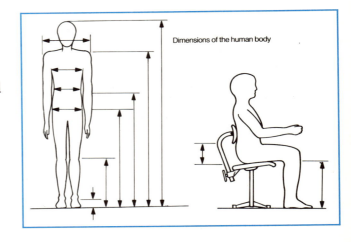

Dimensions of the human body

Appearance – the way things look

Appearance is the way things look. Everything has **appearance** but not everything is pleasing and what seems attractive to one person may seem ugly to another.

Consider the following: lines, shape, form, proportion, pattern, colour, texture, balance.

Pleasing proportion can be achieved by the use of the 'golden ratio'.

Personal qualities of the designer are often referred to as **style**.

The combination of appearance, qualities of touch and style is known as **aesthetics**.

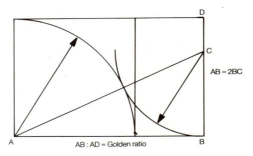

AB = 2BC

AB : AD = Golden ratio

Design and technology in society

Thinking about products

Look at things from different points of view:

a The user.
b The designer.
c The manufacturer.
d People marketing the product.
e Environmental considerations.

Consider the following points

1 What does it do?
2 How well does it do it?
3 What does it cost?
4 How long will it last?
5 Will it go wrong?
6 Can it be mended easily?
7 Why does it look the way it is?
8 What impact will it have on resources, others, the environment?

Product analysis – checklist

Function – Does it perform its task?
Safety – Is it safe to use?
Cost – Is it good value for money?
Manufacture – How was it made?
Efficiency – Will it function well and not waste energy?
Ergonomics – Is it easy to use with least effort or discomfort?
Maintenance – Will it require difficult or expensive servicing?
Social and moral – Does it exploit anyone or have adverse social effects?

Conserving natural resources

World resources are running out. Materials can be recycled.

What can we do about it?

Do you waste materials and natural resources in your CDT projects? Can you think of ways of reusing materials?

1 Plan your work carefully
2 Mark out and cut carefully to size
3 Keep off-cuts for use on smaller projects
4 Use second-hand materials where you can
5 Electrical energy can be conserved by the use of hand processes
6 Do not waste paper. Think of the trees!

Understand what is meant by pollution

The world isn't as 'green' as it might be.

Are you doing anything about it? What else can be done?

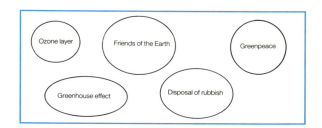

Ozone layer — Friends of the Earth — Greenpeace — Greenhouse effect — Disposal of rubbish

Technology – the application of human knowledge

Energy

Human, sun, water, wind, geothermal, biomass, coal, oil, nuclear.

Careful use of energy.

How do you conserve energy in the home?

Forces

Force:
A push or a pull.

Tension, compression, torsion, bending, shear.
Holding things with forces, e.g. clamps.
Mechanical advantage.

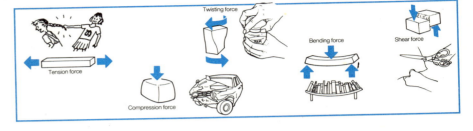

Structures and construction

An arrangement of parts, stability and equilibrium, stiffness and distortion.

Do you understand how a structure can be made stiff, flexible, strong? How are the parts joined together?

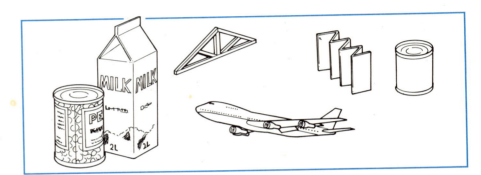

Mechanisms

Levers, links, gears, racks, pulleys, cams, bearings, belts, chains, sprockets.

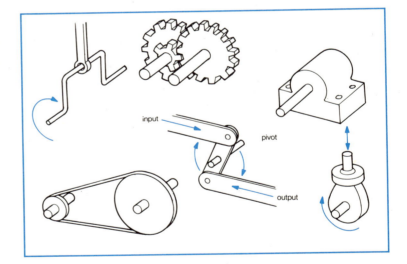

Movement

Linear, reciprocating, rotary, oscillating.

What movements have you used in CDT projects?

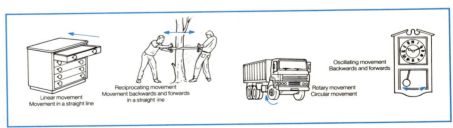

Electricity

Simple circuits, conductivity, resistance, problems and dangers associated with the mains, earthing and fuses.

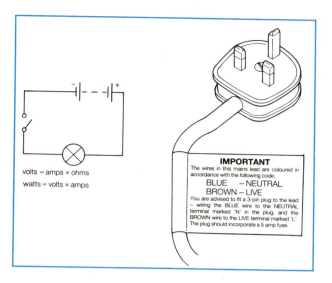

volts = amps × ohms

watts = volts × amps

IMPORTANT
The wires in this mains lead are coloured in accordance with the following code:

BLUE – NEUTRAL
BROWN – LIVE

You are advised to fit a 3-pin plug to the lead – wiring the BLUE wire to the NEUTRAL terminal marked 'N' in the plug, and the BROWN wire to the LIVE terminal marked 'L'. The plug should incorporate a 5 amp fuse.

Controlling things

Switches, variable resistors, water taps, gas valves, rotary control knobs?

Which controllers have you in your house?

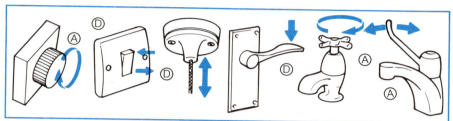

Is modern technology a good or bad thing?

What are the advantages and disadvantages?

Benefits	Disadvantages
It can make life easier and safer for some	Creates stress
Allows greater travel	Produces waste which can pollute
Creates wealth for some	Industrial accidents may be more common
Creates more leisure time	

Tackling written examinations

CDT written examinations require written answers and drawings. It is suggested that you do any drawings in pencil so they can easily be corrected if you make a mistake. The best approach is to answer questions with a combination of written answers and visual annotation. The same question can often be answered in any of three ways. Imagine you have been asked the following question:

Explain how you would join the two pieces of aluminium shown below together.

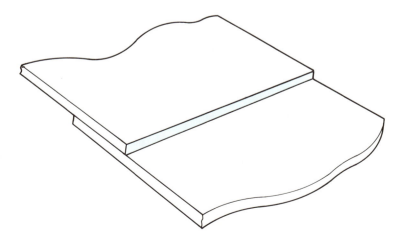

I would drill holes in each part spacing them out evenly about 25 mm apart. I would then put snap head rivets through and using a ball pein hammer, rivet set and snap, I would shape the end of the rivet by hitting it and then shaping it with the rivet snap. The holes and rivets would be 3 mm.

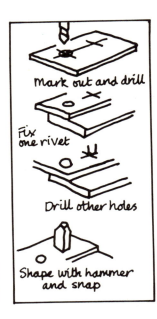

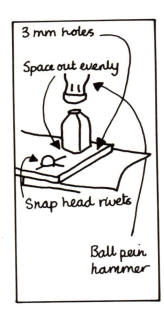

| Written answer | Drawing | Annotated drawing |

Which do you think is the best answer? Which shows what you want to say most clearly? Which answer took least time to do?

It is important to realize that there are frequently no 'right' or 'wrong' answers, only good and poor ones. The worst thing you can do is to write or draw nothing. If you really think you have no idea make a sensible guess. The examiner is there to give you marks and not take them away. Do not be tempted to put down silly answers as this will hardly get the examiner on your side.

Written examinations often consist of two types of question:

1 Short answer questions (usually compulsory).

2 Longer answer questions (often the choice of two from a selection).

Begin by reading through the whole paper marking (in pencil) the ones you think you can answer best.

Alongside each question there will be an indication of how many marks it is worth. If there are few marks then the answer should not be and take very long. If there are more marks then more detail is expected.

Some candidates find it easier to tackle the compulsory questions first. You are sure to find you can answer some of them without much hesitation. The rest may require more thinking. Be careful to balance your time so that you have an appropriate amount of time to spend on each of the questions.

Short answer questions

Short answer questions are set to test your knowledge and to some extent understanding of theoretical facts. Sometimes there will be a 'correct' answer but on many occasions a variety of answers may be allowed. Examiners will give you credit for an intelligent well-reasoned answer which goes some way to answering the question.

Consider the following example. You can adopt a **key word** approach: underlining all the key words.

1 Name a <u>tool(s)</u> with which to mark <u>lines</u> at <u>right angles</u> to the <u>edge</u> of a piece of <u>mild steel</u> strip.

How would you answer this? You might expect that the **correct answer** would be 'Engineer's square' and it is true that this answer would get full marks. However, suppose you didn't know this and answered 'Set square'? This tool could be used and within reason it would enable the job to be done but it wouldn't be the best tool to choose. The examiners would therefore give some credit for this answer. What if you knew the correct answer in terms of the 'look' of the tool but didn't know its name? Suppose you did a simple sketch? In all probability the examiners would give you most of the marks.

When you have answered the question go back and look at the key points. Have you named a <u>tool</u> or <u>tools</u> which will mark <u>lines</u> at <u>right angles</u> to the <u>edge</u> of a piece of <u>mild steel</u> strip? Make sure it is a **tool**; that it marks **lines**; that they are at **right angles**; and that it is suitable for **mild steel**.

Consider the following example which shows answers to a typical short answer question. Each part is to be marked out of three marks: examiner comments and marks are given afterwards.

Material	Marking tool
(a) Acrylic	*Permanent marker pen*
(b) Wood	*Marking knife*
(c) Metal	✓ ✓

Examiner comments

Part **(a)** is perfectly acceptable and deserves full marks.
Part **(b)** is also a good answer and deserves full marks.
Part **(c)** would be worth full marks if the drawings had been a little better. *Marks: 2/3 (two marks out of three).*

Now see how you would get on if having to award marks. Look at the table below and the responses given. Each response is to be marked out of three (a total of 12 marks for the question). Examiner comments and marks are **highlighted by a blue background**.

Complete the table below. Each line links a marking process with materials and suitable tools.

Process	Material	Sketch of tool(s)
(a) Marking lines at right angles to an edge	Bright mild steel	
(b)		

cont'd

Process	Material	Sketch of tool(s)
(c)	Nylon bar for turning	

Examiner comments

Part **(a)** is a good answer. *Full marks.*

Part **(b)** shows some understanding. For full marks the answer should indicate that the lines are marked parallel to an edge and the name of a specific type of material should be given, e.g. Scots Pine. The answer given would get: *Marks: 3/6.*

Part **(c)** is a vague answer and since the introduction to the question had already indicated the questions were about marking processes then this answer is not worth any marks. An answer indicating that the tool is used for marking the centre of the bar was required.

This next question is slightly more difficult and more marks (six) are available for each question. There is also more space available for the answers which suggests more detailed answers are expected.

There are sensible ways of conserving energy in a school workshop. State how an economic use of energy may be achieved in each of the following situations:

(a) Brazing two pieces of mild steel together   *Use less heat*

_____

_____

(b) Buffing the edge of acrylic on a buffing machine   *Clean up with "wet and dry" paper and hand polish first*

(c) Removing waste wood on a sanding disc   _____

Switch off when not in use

_____

Examiner comments

Part **(a)** is a vague answer, which although indicating that the candidate is aware that energy can be wasted through overuse of heat, does not properly answer the question. *Marks: 3/6.*

cont'd

> *A better answer would be:*
> *'Make sure the metal is clean and fluxed so that it brazes first time and there is no need to do it again. Surround with fire bricks in the hearth to avoid loss of heat and use the tip of a blue flame aimed directly at the area of the joint.'*
> *Part (b)* is a perfectly good answer. *Full marks.*
> *Part (c):* obviously this is true but as it applies to **any** piece of electrical equipment it isn't much of an answer. *Marks: 2/6.*
> A better answer would be:
> 'Use a saw to remove most of the waste wood before using the sander. If possible use an edge-cutting tool to obtain the finish avoiding the use of the sander.'

This next question has 10 marks. This suggests that the answer should be fairly detailed.

Two identical components need matching paired holes. Make a simple planning sheet to show how exact matching is achieved.

Plan of action to ensure that the holes are in line:

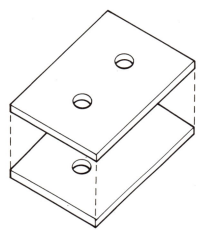

a. Mark out holes

b. Drill holes

c. Switch off machine

> **Examiner comments**
>
> This answer shows a sequence of events but misses out some important details. The candidate could have included, 'Mark out 'centre' of holes', 'Hold in machine vice', 'Drilling the two pieces together', 'Clamp two pieces together or bolt together after drilling first hole'. *Marks: 5/10.*

Summary of short answer questions

- Use the **key word** approach.
- For best marks be specific:
  e.g. 'Junior hacksaw' NOT just 'Saw',
  'Tensol cement' NOT just 'Glue',
  'Bright drawn mild steel' NOT just 'Metal'.
- The space provided gives a clue as to how much information is needed.
- There are frequently a number of suitable answers.
- Attempt all questions and parts which are compulsory.
- Use words **and** drawings if possible.

Longer answer questions

Longer answer questions are intended to test your understanding in a wider context. These questions are often based on a theme. Here are some examples:

LEAG have set questions on the following themes: Research Evaluation, Mini-Enterprise, Mechanisms, Structures, Product Assembly. You are required to answer **two** questions from a selection of **six**.

WJEC has the themes of Materials and Processes *and* Design and Technological Awareness and you must answer **three** questions in total, with at least **one** from each section.

MEG: you must answer **one** compulsory question on Design and Evaluation, **one** compulsory question on Design in Society from a 'researched' theme, and a further **two** structured questions from a selection of **four**.

SEG: you must answer **one** compulsory structured question (it gradually gets harder) based upon a research topic set earlier in the year, and **two** others from a selection of **four**.

NEA has as compulsory set of **five** questions based around a 'researched' theme.

NISEC set **three** compulsory longer answer questions.

The following long answer questions will give you a clue to the quality of answer required by the examiners. The first question is taken from the Design in Society theme set by the MEG.

Games can be of particular importance to people with a disability and can improve their quality of life in a number of ways.

(a) 'Reward' is a very important feature in many games. Explain why this is and describe three games which incorporate some form of reward.

(5 marks)

> **Examiner comments**
>
> A good answer, deserving full marks. *Marks: 2/2.*
> II and III do incorporate reward but not I. *Marks: 2/3.*

Motivation to do better
It's a challenge
It makes a good competition
It gives you satisfaction

I   Jig Saw
II   Basket ball
III   Pass—the—parcel

(b) Give two reasons other that safety, why the materials from which the games are made must be appropriate to a particular disability.

(2 marks)

Soft material if skin is tender
Easily dropped if too light

> **Examiner comments**
>
> Quite good answers but an object could also be dropped if it were too heavy.
> *Marks: 1/2.*

(c) Some children's games are designed to improve hand and eye coordination. Explain what is meant by reference to two examples of games which aim to improve hand/eye coordination.

(4 marks)

Helping your hand to react to what you see

1. Conkers

2. Hand held marble game

(d) Many electronic games possess operating switches which are inappropriate for people with disabilities. Describe how you would modify three switches to help people with one or more of the following disabilities. (3 marks)

(i) Clumsy hand movements   *foot or head switch*

(ii) Poor hand grip   *make larger*

(iii) Limited use of hands/arms but full use of the lower limbs

use a foot pedal

(e) Dominoes, snooker and table-tennis are popular indoor games. Describe the type of disability which would prevent people playing these games with 'normal' equipment. Suggest possible modifications to this equipment to enable disabled people to participate. (6 marks)

Snooker may be difficult
Table tennis might need a smaller table if player was not strong
Dominoes would be difficult if grip poor so make large dominoes

The following two questions also show the responses of two candidates when answering long answer questions. The examiner comments and marks are given after the questions. Try to estimate the mark you would give to the responses of the candidate.

The first question is taken from the WJEC section entitled Design and Technological Awareness.

Ever since the Chernobyl disaster in 1986, 'pressure groups' have been actively campaigning to stop the building of electricity generating schemes that use nuclear fuel.

(a) List two disadvantages of producing electricity using nuclear fuel. (2 marks)

Nuclear power stations are ugly
Nuclear waste is dangerous

(b) List four advantages of producing electricity using nuclear fuel. (4 marks)

Less smoke is produced

It might be cheaper
Fewer people are needed
Less miners are killed underground

(c) List six alternative ways by which electricity can be produced.

(6 marks)

Windmills
Salter-ducks
Hydro-electricity
Water wheels
Batteries
Dams

(d) Choose two of the methods you have named in **(c)** that would be acceptable to the environmentalists, have little risk of causing harm to society and would last indefinitely. Then briefly describe why such methods are not more readily used and why considerable dependence still exists on electricity produced by nuclear fuel.

(8 marks)

1 Windmills — expensive to construct and can spoil the countryside; only work when its windy

2 Salter-duck — they have to be out at sea and as a lot of them are needed it will be expensive to distribute the energy long distances

The second long answer question is taken from a section entitled Mechanisms and was set by LEAG. How well do you think this candidate did?

Simple toy automata (toys involving mechanisms and linked movement) are enjoying a revival. The drawing on the next page shows a pupil's idea for such a toy.

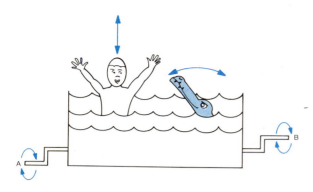

(a) The characters are to be made from sheet material. State a suitable material and its thickness.

    (i) Material ___Plastic___

    (ii) Thickness ___3mm___

                           (3 marks)

(b) Within the base box there will be a mechanical system which makes the swimmer rise and then disappear below the water, when handle **A** is turned. Show how this movement can be achieved.   **(10 marks)**

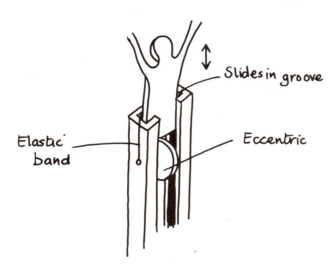

(c) The crocodile rises out of the water in an arc.
(i) Show how the crocodile is fixed to 'make' it move in an arc.

                                  (3 marks)

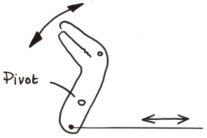

(ii) Show how the crocodile can be made to rise and disappear below the water by turning handle **B**.   **(10 marks)**

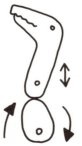

(d) The pupil then decides that two rows of waves are to alternately oscillate to give the impression of movement. Show how this could be done; if necessary a third handle may be added.   **(10 marks)**

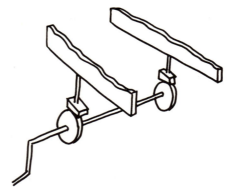

(e) Finally, the pupil realizes that the toy would be greatly improved if all three systems were operated on one handle. Show how this could be achieved.

(14 marks)

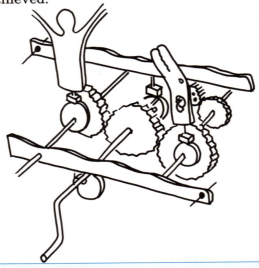

Summary of longer answer questions
- Use the **key word** approach as for short answer questions.
- Answer the correct number of questions.
- Answer ALL parts of each question.
- Each question will usually get harder towards the end.
- Only answer the required number of questions. Some examination groups only give credit for the **first** ones attempted.

Remember: there may be as many marks for each longer question than all the short ones added together.

General hints

Remember: there are frequently no 'right' answers only good ones, except where the question is set to test a very specific piece of knowledge. The only way you can guarantee getting zero marks for a question is to leave it blank.

Where you have a choice of questions, make sure you know how many you have to answer and choose the ones where you can answer the parts which have the most marks.

The early parts of most longer questions are easy and so don't be fooled into starting a question only to find that you can't then do the parts with the most marks.

Plan your time carefully and certainly do not spend too long on those questions which do not have many marks.

If you have any time left go over the paper and make sure you have not made any silly mistakes. You will want to get a high grade and a few marks can make all the difference.

Revision questions

Attempt these questions **before** looking at the suggested answers that start on page 141. All dimensions are in mm, unless otherwise stated. Where dimensions are not shown, use your discretion.

Materials

1 What do you understand by the term 'man made' boards?

(*NEA, 1988*)

2 Name **one** material suitable for each given process.

Process	Specific material
Woodturning	BEECH
Blow moulding	
Hardening and tempering	
Laminating	

(*LEAG, 1990*)

3 Complete the table by naming a specific material.

Generic name	Family	Specific material
Wood	Hardwood	
	Softwood	
Metal	Ferrous	
	Non-ferrous	
Plastic	Thermo	
	Thermosetting	

(*WJEC, 1989*)

4 Draw two sectional forms in which plastics mouldings are available.

(*WJEC, 1990*)

5 Write the full meaning of the abbreviation BDMS.　(*SEG, 1988*)

6 Give an example of a glass reinforced plastics product. (*SEG, 1988*)

7: Long answer question

It has been decided to make a carrier for up to four milk bottles using materials of your choice but including plastic pipe arranged as shown in the diagram below.

(**a**) Show the details of your design solutions to the following problems:

(**i**) A means of supporting the base of the bottles when they are placed in the carrier.

(**ii**) A method of fixing together the four pieces of pipe.

(**iii**) A carrying handle and its attachment to the bottle holders.

(**iv**) A means of preventing birds pecking away the foil bottle caps to get at the milk.

(**b**) Give three reasons, other than cost, for choosing the materials and finish you have used for your design.

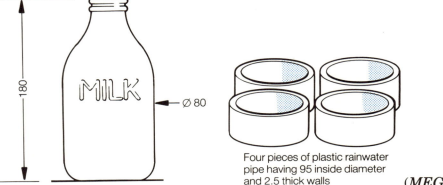

Four pieces of plastic rainwater pipe having 95 inside diameter and 2.5 thick walls

(*MEG, 1988*)

8: Long answer question

The diagram below shows the overall size of five floppy disks for a computer and an outline drawing of a suitable container.

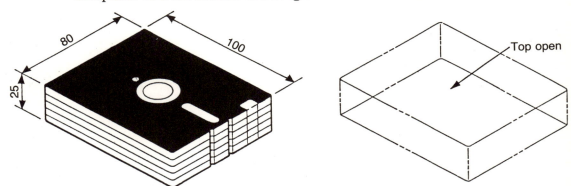

Materials

(**a**) Name two suitable materials for making one container only.

(**b**) Name two suitable materials for making a batch of twenty identical containers.

Processes

(**c**) Choose one of the materials you have named in (**b**) and state a suitable thickness for the (**i**) Sides. (**ii**) Bottom.

(**d**) Show with the aid of sketches a method of joining a long side with one of the short sides.

(**e**) Name a suitable process for making a batch of twenty identical containers.

(**f**) With clear drawings and notes show how twenty containers could be produced. (*WJEC, 1990*)

Manufacturing

9 For each of the materials listed, name a process used to achieve a 90° bend.

Material	Process
Thermoplastic	
Veneers of beech	
Gilding metal	

(*LEAG, 1989*)

10 Name a suitable process that will produce a hollow form, illustrated below, from a plastics material.

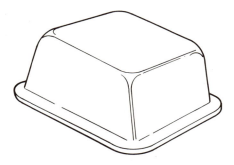

(*WJEC, 1989*)

11 Metals can be heated to red heat and then quenched. Name a metal that would be left hard by this process. (*MEG specimen*)

12 State what you understand by the following terms:
Batch production
One-off

Give one example of an object which has been made by a batch production process and name a suitable means of production.

(*WJEC, 1989*)

13: Long answer question

The residents of an old people's home decided that they would like to identify the corridors by giving them street names. A school mini-enterprise group is to produce designs for realization and locate them in the corridors of the home.

(a) List four aspects that need to be researched before setting about the task of producing the ideas.

(b) State how you would carry out the research:
1 At school
2 At the elderly people's home

(c) Having produced a number of possible designs, how would you establish the 'best' solution?

WORKFORCE	TASKS
Pupil no. 1	
Pupil no. 2	
Pupil no. 3	
Pupil no. 4	
Pupil no. 5	

(d) Assume that 20 are to be produced:
  (i) Give details of a possible design.
  (ii) Name the material(s).
  (iii) Name the process to be used.
  (iv) List and number the operations in each process.
  (v) Having listed the operations and knowing that 20 street signs are to be made and located in the corridors, use the chart on the previous page to plan how a workforce of five pupils can be employed. *(LEAG, 1989)*

Finishing

14 Complete the following table stating the finish which would be appropriate in each case.

Material	Situation	Finish
Softwood window frame	Outside the house	
Marine plywood	Hull of dinghy	
Mild steel rod	Draining rack	
Brass	Outdoor letterbox – to retain its brightness	

(MEG specimen)

15 Select a suitable surface treatment for the following situations:
  (a) Providing a grip on a bar of metal.
  (b) Protecting the surface of a hardwood top of a coffee table.
  (c) Garden seat made from softwood.
  (d) A mild steel milk bottle holder made from 3mm rod.
  (WJEC, 1989)

16 Name a type of applied surface finish that would be suitable for pine panelling in a kitchen. *(SEG, 1988)*

17 Outline a specific 'restoration treatment' for each of the following:

Situation	Restoration treatment
A weathered outdoor wooden seat	
A dull coffee table surface	
A tarnished gilding metal dish	
A scratched acrylic cover	
A rusty metal garden gate	
A chipped wooden toy	

(LEAG, 1990)

18: Long answer question

The diagram below shows the working surface of a computer station. The component marked A is a stand for the visual display unit (VDU television monitor) and a storage space for the keyboard when not in use.

Materials

    (a) Name one specific timber or manufactured board that would be suitable for making the working surface and component A.

    (b) State a suitable thickness for the material.

    (c) State two factors that influence your choice.

Processes

    (d) Describe, with the aid of diagrams, the method of joining:

        (i) The corners of component A.

        (ii) The unit to the working surface of the computer station.

    (e) Name a suitable finish or surface treatment that could be applied to the chosen material.

    (f) State why the finish or treatment is suitable.

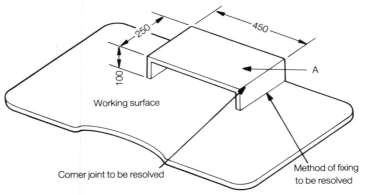

(WJEC, 1989)

Tools and equipment

19 Complete the following table, naming the hand tool you would use to cut curves on the material indicated.

Material	Tool
22 SWG copper sheet	
14 SWG mild steel sheet	
4mm acrylic sheet	
4mm plywood	

(MEG specimen)

20 Name the saw that would be used to remove the shaded portion of the joint shown.

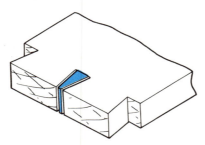

(SEG, 1988)

21 Name the tools you would use for the processes indicated below:

    (a) **(i)** Making the arc.

        (ii) Preventing the marking tool from slipping.

(b) **(i)** Cutting the 18mm diameter holes.
(ii) Cutting along the dotted lines.

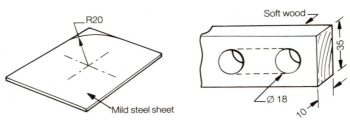

(MEG, 1989)

22: Long answer question

The diagram below shows a block with a 10mm diameter hole through it. The block will form part of a children's construction kit.

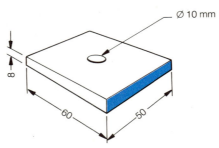

(a) Name a suitable material for the block and give two reasons for your choice.

(b) State two precautions which must be taken when drilling the 10mm diameter hole in your chosen material.

(c) Describe, using notes and sketches, how you would mark out and drill the hole in the block. Your description should include details of the tools and equipment that would be used.

(d) The illustration below shows two line diagrams of the frame of a garden chair. The chair has a folding back. In **(i)** the back is in the upright position. In **(ii)** the back is folded. The frame could be made from either wood or metal.

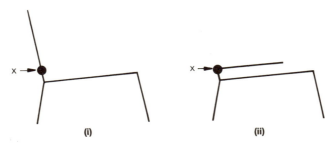

(i) Name either a type of wood or a type of metal from which you would make the chair frame.

(ii) Draw a cross-section through your chosen material and clearly indicate the sizes.

(iii) Design a joint at position X which will allow the backrest to fold as shown in illustration **(ii)**. Draw the joint, showing clearly the detail of the design, and name any components used.

(SEG, 1989)

23 Which of the metalwork lathe tools shown below is correctly set?

(SEG, 1989)

24 Give an explanation of the following terms:

Term	Explanation
Manufactured boards	
Work hardening	
Curing time	

(*LEAG, 1990*)

25 The drawing shows a dome that has been formed from acrylic sheet. Name a production process that you would use to form the dome.

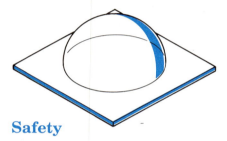

(*SEG, 1988*)

Safety

26 Complete the following chart on safety.

Situation	Precaution	Reason
Pouring molten aluminium in a sand mould	Stand the flask on a surface of sand	To stop an accidental overflow of hot metal spreading
Preparing to drill a piece of material	Remove key from the chuck	
Bending hot metal		To avoid burning hands or clothes
	Open a window	To ensure good ventilation
Preparing to turn material on a lathe	Ask the teacher to check before switching on the power	

(*WJEC, 1989*)

27 Name three features of bathrooms which could cause accidents.

(*NEA, 1988*)

28 State one safety precaution you would take:
    (a) Before switching on a drilling machine.
    (b) When using a 'sanding' machine.
    (c) Whilst mounting a piece of work in a lathe.
    (d) When handling hot metal.   *(LEAG, 1988)*

29 Give an example of a workshop process when you would use:
    (a) Protective eye glasses.
    (b) Face mask for nose and mouth.   *(MEG, 1989)*

Design and technology in society

30: Long answer question

A parent wants to buy a suitable toy for a two–three year old child and has come to you for advice.

    (a) List four features of a well-designed toy.
    (b) Describe briefly how you would assess:
      (i) The suitability of a toy for a two–three year old child.
      (ii) Whether or not a toy was good value for the amount paid.
    (c) List four design or manufacturing features that would be unacceptable in a child's toy.
    (d) Name a national group or organization whose aim is to protect the public from buying goods of unacceptable quality and at worse likely to be very dangerous.
    (e) State how you would show that a toy has been approved and acceptable as suitable for playing with by a child.   *(WJEC, 1989)*

31: Long answer question

The illustration below shows four different solutions produced by pupils in response to a design problem concerned with a desk tidy.

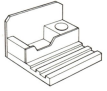

A Wood   **B** Acrylic   **C** Metal   **D** Card flat pack

    (a) All the desk tidies require a suitable finish.
State a suitable finish for each of the designs.
    (b) (i) State the main overall dimensions for the flat pack desk tidy to be made from card.
      (ii) State three vital features for any desk tidy.
      (iii) State two situations where you would select the flat pack desk tidy (card) in preference to others.
    (c) Make a list of four important questions that should be asked when evaluating a desk tidy in use.
    (d) Describe in detail how one of the designs **A**, **B** or **C** could be made.
Use annotated diagrams to illustrate your answer.
    (e) From the illustration above, select the design you find most pleasing, giving your reasons.
    (f) From the illustration above, which design do you consider is the least pleasing to look at, and detail why it fails.   *(LEAG, 1990)*

32: Long answer question

The modern domestic kitchen incorporates features resulting from good design and recent technological innovation. Many of the features are the result of social and economic change.

    (a) The three main services found in most kitchens are water, gas and electricity. Name four items of equipment found in the kitchen which use at least one of these services.
    (b) Manufactured boards and plastics are widely used in most domestic kitchens and have replaced traditional materials such as wood and metal. Give two examples where this has occurred.

(c) Hygiene has always been important in kitchen design. Use two examples to explain how the levels of hygiene have improved.

(d) Kitchen units are increasingly being sold by DIY stores as 'knockdown' units for the consumer to construct and fit.

(i) Give two reasons why units are sold in 'knockdown' form.

(ii) Explain why this could be both an advantage and a disadvantage to the consumer.

(e) The kettle shown below is an example of technological innovation. Explain one aspect of the design which illustrates how the designer has taken into account functional and aesthetic considerations.

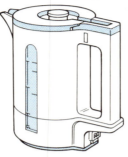

(MEG, 1988)

Technology

33 Compression is one type of force that occurs in many structures and design situations. List three other types of force that can be found in structures.

(NEA, 1988)

34 The drawing shows a simple gear train.

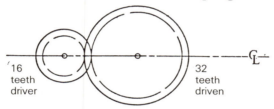

(a) Name the relationship of the speed of the motor driver gear to the speed of the driven gear.

(b) State how many revolutions the driver gear has to rotate to make the driven gear complete one revolution.

(c) Draw an arrangement of gears that will allow:

(i) The driver gear and the driven gear to rotate in the same direction.

(ii) The driver gear to rotate twice as quickly as the driven gear.

(iii) The direction of movement to change through 90°.

(d) Name the type of gear used for (c)(iii).   (WJEC, 1990)

35 Show on the diagram below, how the rotation of shaft A can be used to turn shaft B in the opposite direction.

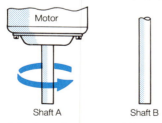

Shaft A   Shaft B   (SEG, 1989)

36 An electric soldering iron is rated at 15 watts and is used in a workshop from a 110 volt supply. Which fuse rating would be most suitable?

3amp   5amp   13amp   (SEG, 1989)

37 What is meant by each of the following? Give an example of each one.

Term	Example	Explanation
Structure		
Framework		
Dynamic forces		

(LEAG, 1989)

38 The diagram below shows the lever mechanism used in a manual typewriter. (The levers in the diagram are shown as outlines and the linkages connecting them are drawn in heavy black lines. The pivots which connect the linkages to the levers are shown as black dots.)

When a key is pressed the type bar strikes the paper.
Show how the mechanism works from the time a key is pressed to the time the type bar strikes the paper.

Illustrate your answer by marking the diagram clearly with:

  (a) An arrow to show the direction of movement of each lever.
  (b) A cross to mark the pivot of each lever.

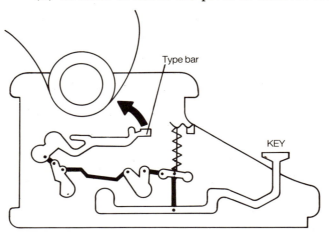

(NEA, 1988)

39 The diagram below shows the shaft of an electric motor (A) which runs at 1000 revs/min driving another shaft (B).

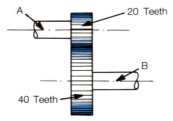

  (a) What is the speed of shaft B?
  (b) State the number of teeth required on the shaft B gearwheel if the shaft is to rotate at 125 revs/min.

(SEG specimen)

40 The drawing shows a tent supported by guy ropes. By means of arrows, indicate the force acting in each of the guy ropes.

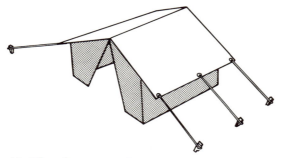

(*SEG, 1988*)

41 The drawing shows a simple lighting circuit. One of the components is 'ringed' in a chain line. Why would the ringed circuit be included in the circuit?

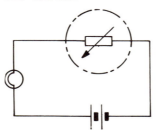

(*SEG, 1988*)

42 The drawing shows a mechanical clamp used to hold down the frame of a vacuum former.

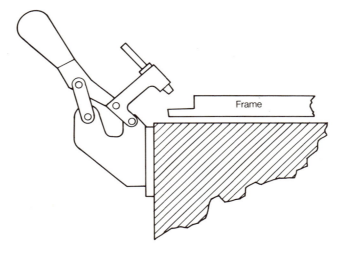

(a) Name the type of mechanism shown.
(b) The clamp is shown in an open position. Redraw the clamp in a closed locked position to show how the frame can be held firmly in place.

(*NEA, 1989*)

Answers to revision questions

There now follow suggested answers to the sample revision questions. After most answers there are also useful hints on how to answer the question and/or alternative responses to the question. Please note that the answers and hints given in this section are entirely those of the author, and that the relevant examination groups accept no responsibility whatsoever for the accuracy or method of working.

Materials

1 Manufactured board such as plywood or blockboard.

Hints: *Always try to give an example*

2 Acrylic.
Carbon steel.
Ash.

Hints: *Make your answers specific and give named examples*

3 Beech.
Scots Pine.
Mild steel.
Copper.
Acrylic.
Polyester resin.

Hints: *Try to be as specific as possible, for example, answering 'bright drawn mild steel'* **not** *just 'steel'*

4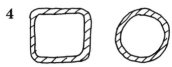

Hints: *Any moulding would do but try to remember where you have seen plastic mouldings – you might even see them in use in the examination room!*

5 Bright drawn mild steel.

Hints: *Make sure you know the difference between this (BDMS) and black mild steel (BMS)*

6 Canoe.

Hints: *You may have used GRP for a school project. You can't expect the examiner to know this so choose a product he or she will know*

7: Long answer question

(a) (i)(ii)(iii)(iv)

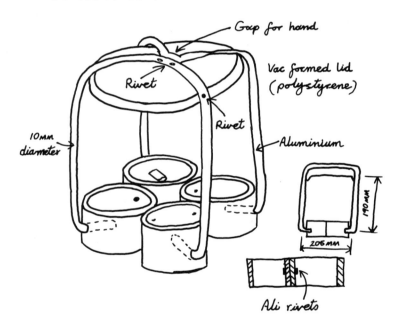

(b) Easily available, resistant to the weather, I have used them before.

Hints: *You could answer part* **(a)** *with one drawing or a series of drawings. Do not mix too many materials together or you may have difficulty joining them. Your drawings should be clear but they don't need to be perfect. Don't be tempted to write down a description when a drawing will do so much better. For* **(b)** *avoid answers like 'they look nice' as it's really a matter of opinion*

8: Long answer question
(a) Aluminium, copper, acrylic, plywood, medium density fibreboard.
(b) Acrylic, rigid polystyrene.
(c) (i) 3mm acrylic.
    (ii) 3mm acrylic (the same).

(d)

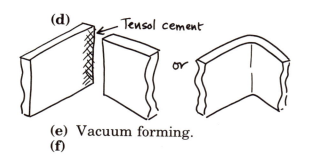

Tensol cement

or

(e) Vacuum forming.

(f)

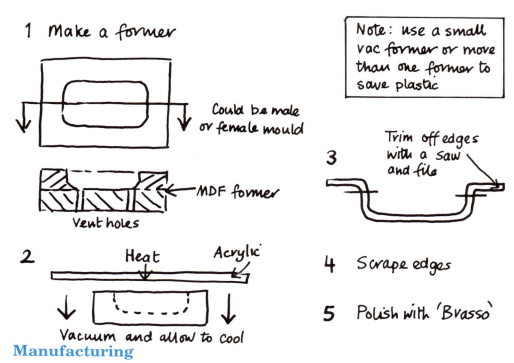

1 Make a former

Could be male or female mould

MDF former

Vent holes

Note: use a small vac former or move than one former to save plastic

3 Trim off edges with a saw and file

2 Heat   Acrylic

Vacuum and allow to cool

4 Scrape edges

5 Polish with 'Brasso'

Manufacturing

9 Strip heater and bend around former.
Laminating in former.
Bend cold after annealing either in vice or folding bars.

Hints: *You cannot get a perfect 90° bend in many materials but the examiner would not expect answers which involved joining two parts to make a right angle. Steam bending might also be appropriate for beech and you could also use bending or a folding machine for gilding metal*

10 Vacuum forming.

Hints: *You could also use the plug and yoke method*

11 Carbon steel.

Hints: *All steel contains carbon and so a better answer would be 'high carbon (or tool) steel'. You may have used high speed steel for cutting tools. It is not hardened in the same way. Don't get them confused*

12 Making a fixed number of an item where it has been possible to set up (specialist tools, etc) a dedicated manufacturing process.

Making one only of an item. Each component is individually made and fitted to others.

Example: wallpaper, which would be manufactured by printing.

13: Long answer question

Questions like this have no exclusive answer. The responses suggested below are some which would gain high marks.

    (a) What the residents would like, the heights of the residents, the amount of light in the corridors, how much money is available, the eyesight of the residents.
    (b) 1 Prepare sketches of ideas and take them to the home. Investigate costs of manufacture.

2 Ask the matron for a budget. Look for suitable fixing places.

(c) Ask the residents. Compare costs.

(d) (i)

(ii) Rigid polystyrene sheet.

(iii) Vacuum forming and hand shaping followed by gluing together.

(iv) 1 Prepare suitable mould.

2 Select polystyrene sheet.

3 Put mould in vacuum forming machine. Place on sheet, switch on heat and vacuum form.

4 Trim to size with knife or coping saw and file.

5 Mark out letters on scrap pieces (different colour) and cut out.

6 Carefully glue letters in place with polystyrene cement. Ensure there is good ventilation.

(v)

WORKFORCE	TASKS		
Pupil no. 1	Make pattern for Vac Former	Operate Vac Former	Fix letters with polystyrene glue
Pupil no. 2		Take out and put in plastic	
Pupil no. 3		Trim plastic to size	
Pupil no. 4	Mark out and shape letters		
Pupil no. 5	Mark out and cut letters		Drill holes

Hints: *Part **(d)** of this question is about organization. Try to think of the details and really imagine **you** are doing it, adding details about 'ventilation' and things like 'wear gloves to remove sheet from vacuum former' will help the examiner to see you really do understand*

Finishing

14 Prime and paint.
Coat with marine grade varnish.
Dip coating with PVC.
Lacquer with clear varnish.

15 (a) Knurl on lathe.

(b) Cellulose varnish.

(c) Creosote or wood preservative.

(d) Paint or dip coating.

Hints: *There are usually a variety of answers for questions like these. Try to make sure each response is different, e.g. you could have written 'varnish' as the finish for each of the materials in question 14 but you wouldn't have got full marks!*

16 Polyurethane varnish.

Hints: *Also giving a reason such as 'it can be cleaned and it protects the pine from steam' would ensure full marks*

17 Rub down with glasspaper and use a weather resistant finish such as wood preservative.
Rub down with steel wool. Blow away dust and lacquer with cellulose.
Polish with a metal polish such as 'Silvo' using a soft cloth.
Rub with a fine acrylic polish and buff on a soft, clean (lamb's wool) mop.
File away rust or treat with a rust remover. Repaint with Hamerite.
Glasspaper, smooth and seal with a wood sealer and paint or varnish the required colour. Must be non-toxic.

Hints: *For best marks you must give a two-stage treatment, i.e. preparation **and** finish*

18: Long answer question

    (a) Plywood.
    (b) 12mm.
    (c) Not too expensive, will not warp.
    (d) (i)

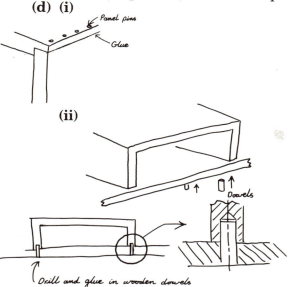

    (e) Polyurethane varnish.
    (f) Improves appearance and would be easy to clean.

Hints: *Questions like this are not difficult providing you can produce neat drawings. Be careful to note that question **(a)** requires the naming of a specific timber suitable for the working surface **and** component A*

Tools and equipment

19 Piercing saw (fine toothed).
Abrafile.
Hacksaw and file.
Coping saw.

Hints: *Try to name a different tool for each material. It may be necessary to name two tools, 'coping saw' and 'file' might be a better answer for 4mm plywood. You may have used a rasp but it would not be suitable for 4mm plywood*

20 Coping saw.

Hints: *Most people would use a coping saw but you might get marks for stating 'fretsaw'*

21 **(a)** **(i)** Centre punch.
　　　　(ii) Dividers.
　　(b) **(i)** Brace and centre bit.
　　　　(ii) Coping saw.

22: Long answer question

(a) Birch plywood: strong in all directions, can be varnished.

(b) Mark out carefully for accuracy, secure material to drilling table before drilling to prevent material from turning and to help produce a clean hole.

(c)

NOTES	SKETCHES
Mark out with pencil using tri-square and marking gauge. Secure on drilling machine. Drill with 10mm Twist drill. Make sure drill is secure and wear goggles Gently clean up with glasspaper. Sand along the grain.	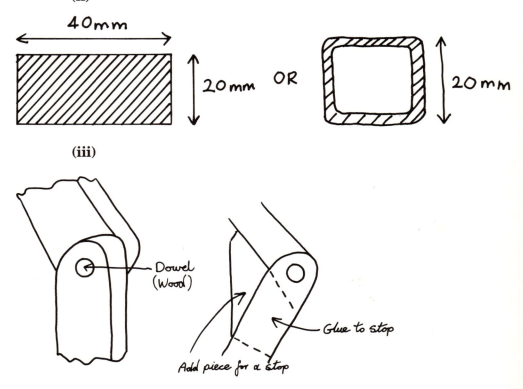

(d) **(i)** Beech, or square mild steel tube.
　　(ii)

40mm ← → 20mm OR 20mm

(iii)

Dowel (Wood)

Add piece for a stop

Glue to stop

23 (iii)

Hints: *All cutting tools for the lathe must be set so that the cutting edge is level with the centre of the work. Too high and they rub. Too low and they dig in. Either way they don't cut cleanly*

24 Flat boards that are made from several pieces of wood or veneers, e.g. plywood.

Some metals such as aluminium and copper get hard when beaten with a hammer.

The time it takes a liquid resin to become a solid material.

Hints: *Explain what the term means* **and** *give an example*

25 Blow moulding.

Hints: *You could of course use a vacuum former or the plug and yoke method but since you would not want any surface damage to the dome then blow moulding would be best. You could mention that the vacuum former can be used in reverse*

Safety

26 So the key does not fly off.
Wear leather apron and gloves.
Casting with polyester resin.
To avoid accidents.

Hints: *Try to think of all the possible dangers. If you haven't experienced the process named then make a sensible guess*

27 Slipping on a wet tiled floor, touching electrical appliances, getting into a bath without testing the temperature of the water.

Hints: *This question was set following research on the topic and so the examiners would not expect 'general' answers which could apply to other situations, e.g. 'it might be hot', 'you might slip'*

28 (a) Remove the chuck key from the chuck so that it will not fly off and hit someone.
(b) Wear goggles to prevent the dust going into your eyes.
(c) Check that the mains power is switched off.
(d) Wear protective clothing so that you do not get burnt. Leather apron and gloves.

Hints: *A general answer will only gain half marks. For full marks you must make the answers relate directly to the task*

29 (a) Drilling on a pillar drill, using a grinder or any situation where eyes are at risk from flying swarf.
(b) Sanding on a disc sander or spray painting.

Hints: *There are obviously many other precautions. Examiners so frequently ask questions about safety you would be foolish not to know the safety precautions for CDT*

Design and technology in society

30: Long answer question

(a) Strong, no sharp edges, non-toxic, interesting or amusing to play with.
(b) (i) Ask parents of two–three year olds, let some two–three year olds play with it and observe and record how they get on.
(ii) Compare cost with similar products on the market, keep a record of how long it lasts and how much it occupies two–three year olds compared with other similar products. See if it is recommended as good value in a Consumers' Association publication.
(c) Unsafe, difficult to manufacture, uses expensive materials, difficult to package.
(d) The Consumers' Association.
(e) British Standards Institution's 'Kitemark'.

Hints: *This question is about analysing products. Have a look at the Consumers' Association's magazine Which?*

31: Long answer question

(a) Design **A**: Coloured stain and varnish.
Design **B**: Polish the edges only.
Design **C**: Rub with steel wool.
Design **D**: Spray on lacquer.

(b) **(i)** Length: 150mm. Width: 150mm. Depth: 150mm.
(ii) Must hold pens, pencils, rubbers etc, contents must be easily identified, contents must be easy to remove and replace.
(iii) Where the desk tidy is to be posted to a friend, where a lot are made and they need to be stored in a confined space.

(c) Does it hold all the items? Does it keep them separate? Are they easy to put in and take out? Does it stand up?

(d)

B 1 Cut acrylic to size
2 Round corners
3 Polish edges

4 Draw with felt pen lines where bends are to take place

5 Centres for holes

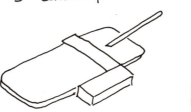

6 Bend 1 on a strip heater
See section view in 9

7 Drill holes

Clamp
Clamp

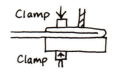

8 Saw cut slot

Vice

9 Heat bend
bends 2, 3, 4 and 5

Bend 2
Bend 1
Bend 3
Bend 4
Bend 5

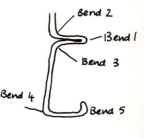

(e) **D.** This can be folded flat. The sides can have useful information, e.g. a calendar. Because it is quick and easy to make it can be easily replaced.

(f) **C.** The pens and pencils are all grouped together in the centre and those in the holes of the base stick out and get in the way. Not a very tidy desk tidy and is limited to pens and pencils.

Hints: **(a)** *Try to select a **different** finish for each desk tidy*
(b) (i) *Any answer within a reasonable range would do – try measuring a pencil to get some idea of size*
(ii) *The feature must be specific and not general. 'Cost', 'correct materials', 'suitable colour' are not likely to gain much credit*
(iii) *Imagine that you try to sell 100 of them to a shop. Think how you would persuade them that your selected design was the best*
(c) *The answer must relate to **any** desk tidy and not a specific design*
(d) *It's more important to mention all the stages than to make the drawings look too artistic*
(e) *'Pleasing' does not only mean appearance – you should bear this in mind when answering this part*
(f) *This time pleasing is more identifiable as 'appearance'*

32: Long answer question

(a) Cooker, dishwasher, washing machine, food mixer.
(b) Melamine coated chipboard for worktops and not solid wood, plastic sinks instead of stainless steel.

(c) Most fresh food is now kept in the fridge, dishwashing machine ensures thorough cleaning of cutlery and crockery, food containers do not have dirt traps (corners or ledges).

(d)(i) Easy to transport, less storage space needed at the warehouse.

(ii) Advantage: keeps costs down. Disadvantage: Standard units will not fit an irregular shaped kitchen.

(e) The vertical handle is easy to hold and allows pouring. The proportions of the space between body and handle are in harmony with rest of kettle.

Hints: *Questions like this draw upon your general technological understanding. No one would expect you to have learned about kitchens and kettles and so the level of answer does not expect a great deal of detail. Try however to make your answer as full as possible and do not repeat information*

Technology

33 Tension, torsion, bending.

Hints: *Another answer could have been 'shear'*

34 (a) Gear ratio.

(b) Two.

(c) (i)

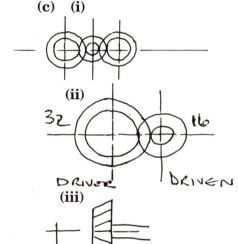

(ii)

32   16

DRIVER   DRIVEN

(iii)

(d) Bevel gear.

Hints: **(a)/(b)** *When answering questions involving gears work out the answer and then work backwards and see if you get back to the same starting point*

(c) (i) *The middle gear is called an idler gear and all it does is reverse the direction of the motion*

(ii) *The gear ratio of this one is 32 : 16 = 2*

(iii) *There are other methods, such as worm and worm wheel, but this one maintains the same speed of rotation*

(d) *These are sometimes called mitre gears*

35 Pulleys with a crossed belt.

Hints: *Gears could of course be used but it would not be appropriate for such a simple situation*

36 3amp fuse.

Hints: *The actual current can be calculated from the equation:*

power (watts) = potential difference (volts) × current (amps)

$15 = 110 × current$

$\dfrac{15\ amps}{110} = current$

$$current = \frac{3}{20} \ amps$$

You should therefore use the smallest value fuse available greater than the above value

37 A wooden box. An arrangement of parts.
A picture frame. A material that encloses a space.
A ball thrown in the air. Moving forces.

Hints: *Make sure you are familiar with the terms used in technology and always be prepared to quote examples*

38 (a) (b)

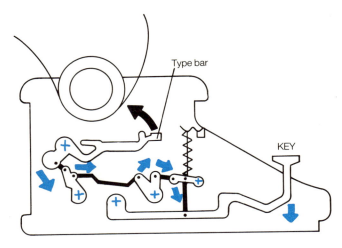

Hints: *You may find this one difficult. Begin at the key and work carefully towards the type. Remember, every lever must have a pivot, a place where it is pulled or pushed and a place where it pushes or pulls. They must all three be in different places. Whenever you need to work out a mechanical system it is often easier to start with the required **output** and work back to the necessary **input***

39 (a) 500 revs/min.
   (b) 160 teeth

Hints: *The motor will go faster than the shaft B. Every 20 teeth of the motor shaft will move the shaft B only half a turn. It will take two turns of the motor shaft for the shaft B to turn once. Therefore, if the motor turns at 1000 revs/min then the shaft B will turn at half that speed, namely 500 revs/min.*
If shaft B rotates even slower then it will need to have a gear with even more teeth. Since the ratio of speed has to be 1000:125 or 8:1 then the new gears must be in the ratio 1:8 or 20:160

40

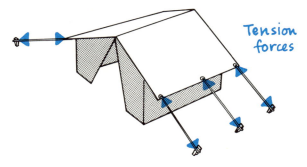

Hints: *It can be difficult to remember which way the arrows go. If in doubt leave them out and say if the ropes will be pulled (in tension) or pushed (in compression)*

41 To vary the brightness of the lamp.

Hints: *Putting any resistance into the circuit will make the current less and the lamp will be dimmer. Because this is a 'variable resistor' the amount of current can be changed and hence the brightness of the lamp*

42 (a) Toggle mechanism.

   (b)

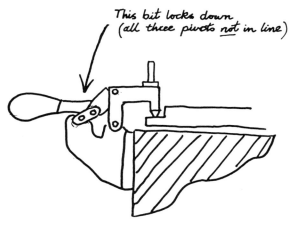

Hints: *Toggles can be difficult to understand. Have a look at other examples such as a 'mole' wrench or the clamps on the vacuum former at school*

Appendices

This section is made up of four parts:

Appendix 1: Summary of examination syllabuses
Appendix 2: Examination groups: addresses
Appendix 3: Data sheets
Appendix 4: Checklists and checkcharts

Summary of examination syllabuses

Breakdown of syllabuses

	LEAG	MEG	NEA	SEG	WJEC	NISEC
COURSEWORK	Selection from 4 terms' work	Selection from 4 terms' work	Selection from 3 terms prior to examinations	Selection from 3 terms prior to examinations	Selection from 11 months' work	Selection from 5 terms' work
WRITTEN EXAMINATION	2 hours	2¼ hours	1¾ hours	2 hours	2 hours	2 hours
DESIGN PAPER	No time limit	—	Research: March—examination Examination: 1¾ hours	Research: 6-8 hours Examination: 2 hours	3 hours	2 hours
DESIGN PROJECT	Autumn term—end of March	December—1st March	—	—	—	—
REALIZATION AND EVALUATION PROJECT	Minimum of 5 hours and maximum of any time may be used between March and early May	Maximum of 20 hours	—	—	—	—

Breakdown of marks

	LEAG	MEG	NEA	SEG	WJEC	NISEC
COURSEWORK	40	30	50	50	50	50
WRITTEN EXAMINATION	30	30	20	25	30	20
DESIGN PAPER	—	—	30	25	20	30
DESIGN AND REALIZATION	30	40	—	—	—	—

All figures as percentage of total marks

Examination groups: addresses

LEAG – London East Anglian Group

London	University of London School Examinations Board Stewart House, 32 Russell Square, London WC1B 5DN (071-636 8000)
LREB	London Regional Examinations Board Stewart House, 32 Russell Square, London WC1B 5DN
EAEB	East Anglian Examinations Board The Lindens, Lexden Road, Colchester CO3 3RL (0206 549595)

MEG – Midland Examining Group

Cambridge	University of Cambridge Local Examinations Syndicate Syndicate Buildings, 1 Hills Road, Cambridge CB1 2EU (0223 61111)
O & C	Oxford and Cambridge Schools Examination Board 10 Trumpington Street, Cambridge CB2 1QB and Elsfield Way, Oxford OX2 8EP
SUJB	Southern Universities' Joint Board for School Examinations Cotham Road, Bristol BS6 6DD
WMEB	West Midlands Examinations Board Norfolk House, Smallbrook Queensway, Birmingham B5 4NJ
EMREB	East Midland Regional Examinations Board Robins Wood House, Robins Wood Road, Aspley, Nottingham NG8 3RL

NEA – Northern Examining Association (*Write to your local board.*)

JMB	Joint Matriculation Board (061-273 2565) Devas Street, Manchester M15 6EU (*also for centres outside the NEA area*)
ALSEB	Associated Lancashire Schools Examining Board 12 Harter Street, Manchester M1 6HL
NREB	Northern Regional Examinations Board Wheatfield Road, Westerhope, Newcastle upon Tyne NE5 5JZ
NWREB	North-West Regional Examinations Board Orbit House, Albert Street, Eccles, Manchester M30 0WL
YHREB	Yorkshire and Humberside Regional Examinations Board Harrogate Office — 31 – 33 Springfield Avenue, Harrogate HG1 2HW Sheffield Office — Scarsdale House, 136 Derbyshire Lane, Sheffield S8 8SE

SEG – Southern Examining Group

AEB	The Associated Examining Board Stag Hill House, Guildford GU2 5XJ (0483 506506)
Oxford	Oxford Delegacy of Local Examinations Ewert Place, Summertown, Oxford OX2 7BZ
SREB	Southern Regional Examinations Board Eastleigh House, Market Street, Eastleigh SO5 4SW
SEREB	South-East Regional Examinations Board Beloe House, 2 – 10 Mount Ephraim Road, Tunbridge Wells TN1 1EU
SWEB	South-Western Examinations Board 23 – 29 Marsh Street, Bristol BS1 4BP

WJEC – Wales

WJEC	Welsh Joint Education Committee 245 Western Avenue, Cardiff CF5 2YX (0222 561231)

NISEC – Northern Ireland

NISEC	Northern Ireland Schools Examinations Council Beechill House, 42 Beechill Road, Belfast BT8 4RS (0232 704666)

(The boards to which you should write are underlined in each case.)

Data sheets

Useful measurements and dimensions

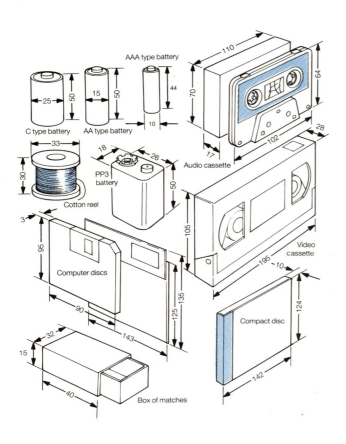

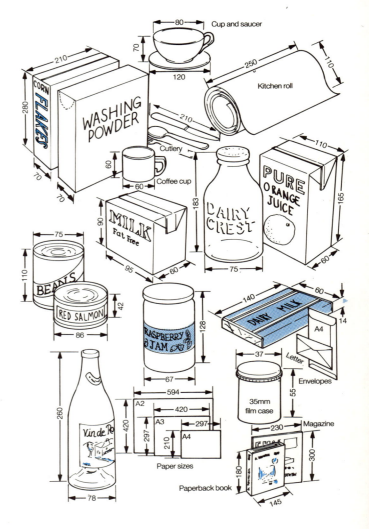

Quick reference British Standards drawing conventions

Electrical and electronic symbols

LINES USED IN TECHNICAL DRAWING

The table below shows the main lines used in technical drawing, and where you use them.

— Thick continuous line: outlines and edges

— Thin, faint continuous line: construction, projection and dimension lines, hatching and sectioning

- - - - - Even dashes: hidden details and edges

— — — Long chain line: centre lines

DIMENSIONING

Dimensions have to be clearly shown on technical drawings. The usual way of doing this is to draw dimension lines and to write the dimension above the middle of the line. Below you can find out about special methods used to dimension circles, radius curves and angles.

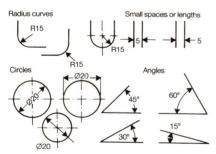

Radius curves

Small spaces or lengths

Circles

Angles

Datum dimensioning

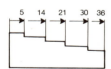

The datum line is marked with a filled-in dot

To show a number of dimensions along one line, measure all the lengths from one end (called the datum line), as this reduces the chance of errors building up. Each of the dimensions shows the distance from the datum line to that point.

ENGINEERING CONVENTIONS

The drawings below show the conventional ways of representing standard features on engineering drawings.

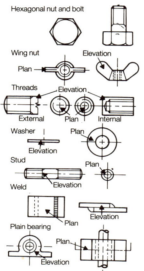

Hexagonal nut and bolt

Wing nut — Plan / Elevation

Threads — Elevation, External, Plan, Internal

Washer — Plan, Elevation

Stud — Plan, Elevation

Weld

Plain bearing — Plan, Elevation

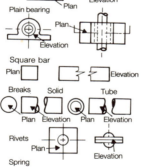

Square bar — Plan, Elevation

Breaks — Solid — Tube — Plan, Elevation

Rivets — Plan, Elevation

Spring — Compression, Tension

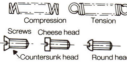

Screws — Cheese head — Countersunk head — Round head

Materials
- Metal
- Wood
- Glass
- Marble
- Water

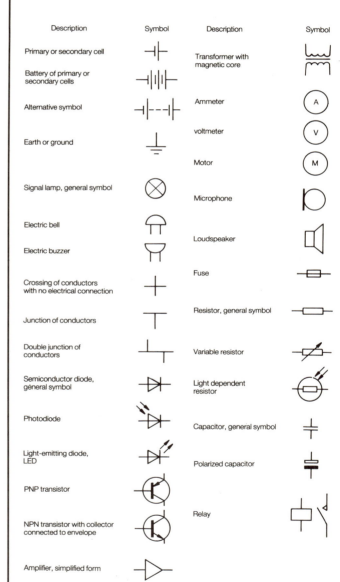

Description	Symbol	Description	Symbol
Primary or secondary cell		Transformer with magnetic core	
Battery of primary or secondary cells			
Alternative symbol		Ammeter	A
Earth or ground		voltmeter	V
		Motor	M
Signal lamp, general symbol		Microphone	
Electric bell			
Electric buzzer		Loudspeaker	
Crossing of conductors with no electrical connection		Fuse	
Junction of conductors		Resistor, general symbol	
Double junction of conductors		Variable resistor	
Semiconductor diode, general symbol		Light dependent resistor	
Photodiode		Capacitor, general symbol	
Light-emitting diode, LED		Polarized capacitor	
PNP transistor			
NPN transistor with collector connected to envelope		Relay	
Amplifier, simplified form			

Anthropometric data

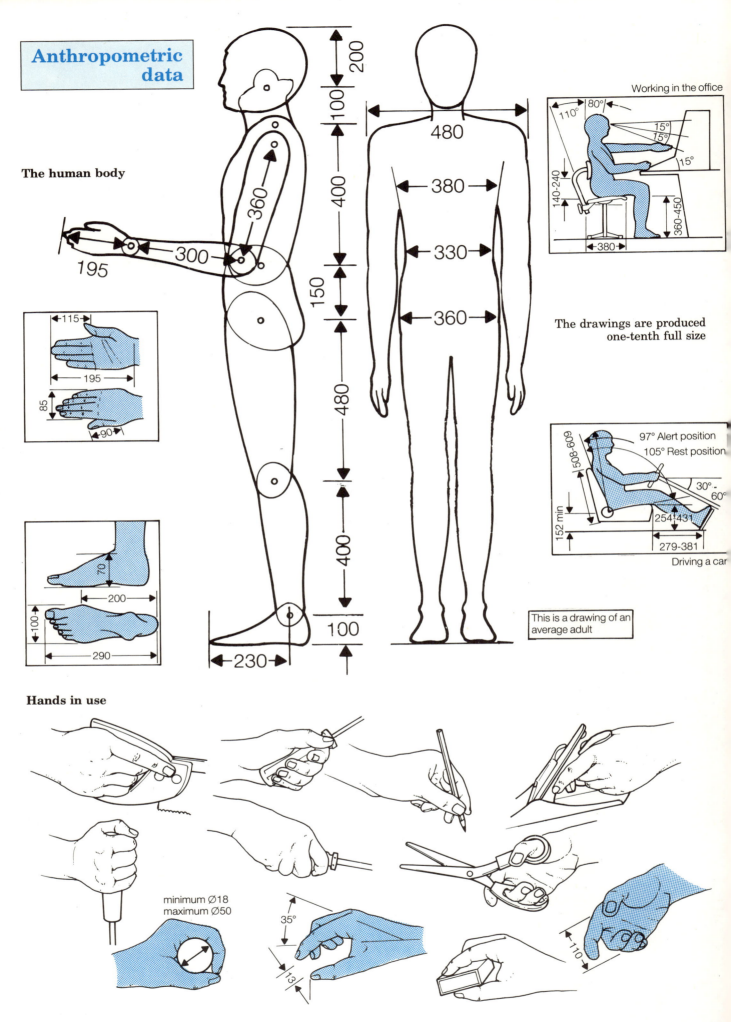

The human body

195
360
300

115
195
85
90

70
200
100
290
230
100

200
100
400
150
480
400
480
380
330
360

Working in the office
110° 80°
15°
15°
15°
140-240
360-450
380

The drawings are produced
one-tenth full size

508-609
97° Alert position
105° Rest position
30° - 60°
254-431
152 min
279-381

Driving a car

This is a drawing of an
average adult

Hands in use

minimum Ø18
maximum Ø50

35°
13
110

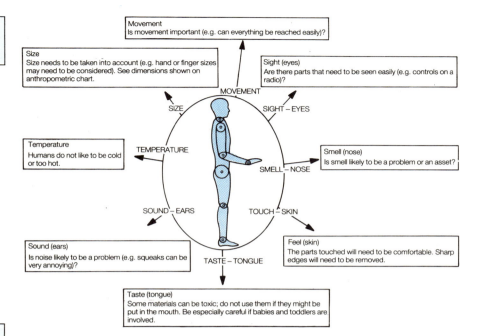

Movement
Is movement important (e.g. can everything be reached easily)?

Size
Size needs to be taken into account (e.g. hand or finger sizes may need to be considered). See dimensions shown on anthropometric chart.

Sight (eyes)
Are there parts that need to be seen easily (e.g. controls on a radio)?

Temperature
Humans do not like to be cold or too hot.

Smell (nose)
Is smell likely to be a problem or an asset?

Feel (skin)
The parts touched will need to be comfortable. Sharp edges will need to be removed.

Sound (ears)
Is noise likely to be a problem (e.g. squeaks can be very annoying)?

Taste (tongue)
Some materials can be toxic; do not use them if they might be put in the mouth. Be especially careful if babies and toddlers are involved.

Prices of materials

This is a selection of the more commonly used materials.
All prices are pence for 300mm lengths or 300mm × 100mm sheets.

Material	Sheet					Rod ●				Square ■				Strip ▬					Tube ○			
	1.5mm	4mm	6mm	12mm	18mm	4mm	6mm	12mm	20mm	12mm	20mm	25mm	50mm	12×3	20×3	12×25	25×50	50×75	12mm	15mm	20mm	25mm
Mild steel	40	X	X	X	X	4	6	25	61	35	93	X	X	9	15	X	X	X	17	18	25	36
Brass	175	X	X	X	X	12	24	90	199	125	273	X	X	41	58	X	X	X	75	91	107	X
Aluminium	53	X	X	X	X	7	12	44	97	50	X	X	X	14	20	X	X	X	33	44	51	72
Acrylic	27	38	75	X	X	18	25	47	145	X	X	X	X	X	X	X	X	X	X	57	89	115
Nylon	X	X	X	X	X	15	43	102	X	X	X	X	X	X	X	X	X	X	X	X	X	X
Softwood (pine)	X	X	X	36	45	X	X	X	X	X	X	12	45	X	X	6	35	70	X	X	X	X
Hardwood	X	X	X	50	63	X	X	X	X	X	X	25	85	X	X	10	45	X	X	X	X	X
Plywood (birch)	X	10	15	25	37	X	X	X	X	X	X	X	X	X	X	X	X	X	X	X	X	X
MDF	X	9	16	21	X	X	X	X	X	X	X	X	X	X	X	X	X	X	X	X	X	X

Note: some materials are still only available in Imperial sizes. Where this occurs the nearest metric equivalents have been quoted.

X: indicates materials not normally available or used for school projects

Assorted materials

Veneered chipboard (mahogany)	25p
Tin plate (.43mm)	59p
Rigid polystyrene sheet	
0.5mm	6p
1.0mm	12p
2.0mm	23p
Hardboard 3.2mm	5p
4.8mm	7p
Copper sheet 1.5mm	183p
Copper tube 15.0mm	143p
Casting aluminium per kg	257p
Styrofoam (300mm × 100mm × 100mm)	50p

Plasticine – per pack		125p
Studding	6.0mm	23p
	4.0mm	53p
Copper clad PCB board		140p

Assorted fastenings and fittings

12mm × No 4 woodscrew	.5p
20mm × No 6 woodscrew	.7p
25mm × No 8 woodscrew	1.1p
50mm × No 10 woodscrew	2p

25mm × 4mm machine screw		2.5p
25mm × 6mm machine screw		4p
6mm nuts (steel)		.8p
4mm nuts (steel)		.6p
Pop rivets (⅛ in)		2p
Butt hinges (steel)	25mm	21p
Butt hinges (steel)	50mm	25p
Butt hinges (brass)	32mm	72p

cont'd overleaf

cont'd

Butt hinges
(brass) 50mm 115p
Knockdown fittings 10p
Modesty blocks 4p

Finishing materials

Glasspaper – per sheet 7p
Emery cloth – per sheet 37p
Varnish (lacquer) – one coat
300mm × 100mm 1p

Paint – two coats
300mm × 100mm 1p

Electronic materials

Insulated connecting wire 1p
Resistors (½ watt) 1p
Transistors BC108 12p
BFY51 18p
LED 6p
LDR 60p
Preset resistor 6p
Small value capacitors 3p

6V lamp and holder 29p
Miniature electric motor 50p
Buzzer 50p
PP3 battery (imported) 35p
PP3 battery clip 5p
AA battery (alkaline) 28p
AA battery holder 10p
Control knob 35p
Solder (300mm) 10p

Useful addresses

Useful and informative information about design

The Design Council
28 Haymarket
London SW1Y 4SU

British Standards Institute
Education Section
2 Park Street
London W1A 2BS

Design for younger children

Community Service Volunteers
237 Pentonville Road
London W1 9NJ

Toys

Geffrye Museum
Kingsland Road
London E2 8EA

Information about Alternative Technology

The Centre for Alternative
Technology
Machynlleth
Powys
Wales

Plastics materials

Trylon Ltd
Thrift Street
Wollaston
Northants NN9 7QJ

Metals and hardware

Heward and Dean Limited
Schools Equipment Division
90 West Green Road
London N15 4SR

Small quantities of materials and mechanical and electrical components

K R Whiston Limited
New Mills
Stockport
Greater Manchester SK12 4PT

Electronic and mechanical components

Proops Distributors Ltd
Heybridge Estate
Castle Road
London NW1 8TD

Electronic components

Maplin Electronic Supplies
PO Box 3
Rayleigh
Essex SS6 2BR

Rapid Electronics
Heckworth Close
Severalls Industrial Estate
Colchester
Essex CO4 4TB

R S Components
PO Box 99
Corby
Northants NN17 9RS

Technology

Durr-Technik
7 West Road
Woolston
Southampton
Hampshire SO2 9AH

Checklists and checkcharts

1 Research chart
Finding information to help you with your project

What kind of info?
Choose one or more of these

	Easy
	Not so easy

Background information	Ideas	Evidence to prove a theory	Gaps in the market	Guidance with an idea	Technical information	Other sources of information
Textbook	Section Five of this book	Ask your teacher	Ask your parents	Ask your teacher	Ask your teacher	Teachers
CDT library	Look in textbooks	Ask other students	Ask friends	Telephone local tradesmen	Ask the technician	Bibliographies
School library	CDT resources	Questionnaires	Visit local shops	Make local visits	Textbooks	School office
Encyclopaedias	School library	Interviews	Use a questionnaire	Write letters to specialists	Catalogues *Timber, RS, Rapid*	School kitchens
Books at home	Comics and magazines	Write letters	Keep your eyes open	Arrange visits to factories	Data sheets	Caretaker
Public library	Ask parents and friends				Telephone suppliers	Sports clubs
Local shops	Public library				Public library	Travel agents
Telephone calls	Keep your eyes open				British Standards	Professional organizations
Write letters	Specialist shops for products to improve				Write to suppliers	Museums

2 A sample letter

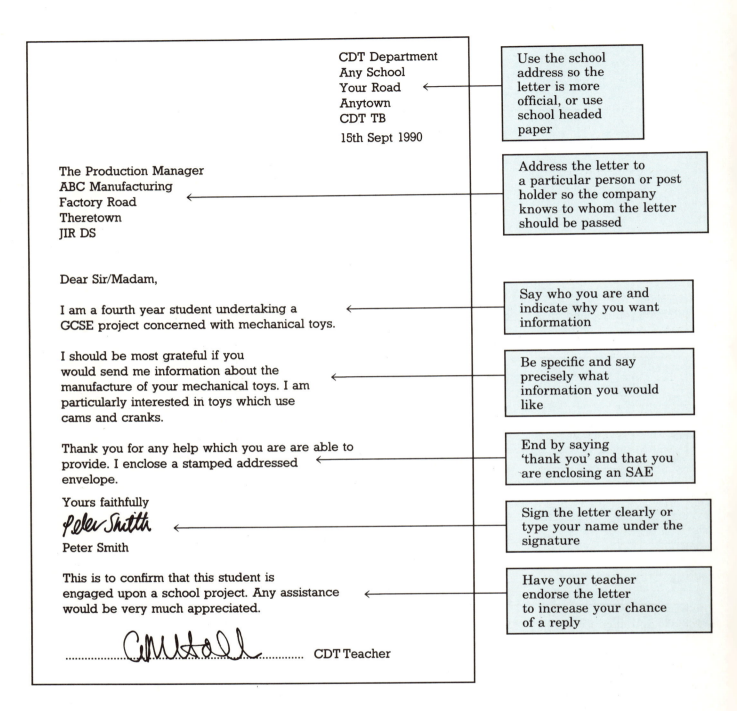

CDT Department
Any School
Your Road
Anytown
CDT TB

15th Sept 1990

> Use the school address so the letter is more official, or use school headed paper

The Production Manager
ABC Manufacturing
Factory Road
Theretown
JIR DS

> Address the letter to a particular person or post holder so the company knows to whom the letter should be passed

Dear Sir/Madam,

I am a fourth year student undertaking a GCSE project concerned with mechanical toys.

> Say who you are and indicate why you want information

I should be most grateful if you would send me information about the manufacture of your mechanical toys. I am particularly interested in toys which use cams and cranks.

> Be specific and say precisely what information you would like

Thank you for any help which you are are able to provide. I enclose a stamped addressed envelope.

> End by saying 'thank you' and that you are enclosing an SAE

Yours faithfully

Peter Smith

> Sign the letter clearly or type your name under the signature

This is to confirm that this student is engaged upon a school project. Any assistance would be very much appreciated.

> Have your teacher endorse the letter to increase your chance of a reply

.... CDT Teacher

Hints for writing a letter

1 *Make sure it is polite*
2 *Check spelling*
3 *Be careful with handwriting or better still type or use a word processor*

3 Specification checklist
Use this before you start designing

	Project 1	Project 2	Project 3
Have you stated what your project is intended to do?	○	○	○
Have you stated the minimum and maximum sizes if they matter?	○	○	○
Does your project have to hold or contain anything? Say exactly what it must contain	○	○	○
Have you decided on a maximum cost for your project?	○	○	○
Has your project to be completed in a specific amount of time?	○	○	○
Are there specific environment requirements, such as being waterproof?	○	○	○
Are there specific safety considerations?	○	○	○
Are there any restrictions of equipment or materials?	○	○	○
Do you need to comply with any legal requirements?	○	○	○
Are looks important or does the appearance matter?	○	○	○

4 Costings checklist

Use this when deciding upon your best idea
and when working out the cost of a project

	Project 1	Project 2	Project 3
Have you considered the cost of the materials?	◯	◯	◯
Have you considered the standard sizes and quantities in which you can purchase your materials?	◯	◯	◯
Minimum order charges? One electronics supplier charges a minimum of £15.00	◯	◯	◯
Postage, packing and other delivery costs?	◯	◯	◯
Polishes, paints and other finishes?	◯	◯	◯
Glasspaper, emery cloth, other abrasives, cleaners and solvents?	◯	◯	◯
Energy to run machinery and equipment?	◯	◯	◯
Heating and lighting of the workshop?	◯	◯	◯
Value Added Tax (VAT)?	◯	◯	◯

5 Details checklist
Use this whilst developing your ideas

	Project 1	Project 2	Project 3
Are all materials you intend to use named?	◯	◯	◯
Will you be able to shape the materials as you intend?	◯	◯	◯
Have you stated suitable methods of joining the parts together?	◯	◯	◯
Will it be safe in use: sharp edges, corners, too heavy, toxic materials?	◯	◯	◯
Will the materials have the appropriate mechanical properties?	◯	◯	◯
Are the sizes of materials quoted available as standard sizes?	◯	◯	◯
Are the materials available?	◯	◯	◯
Can anything be done in a simpler or easier way?	◯	◯	◯
Is there a cheaper way to do things or could you use cheaper materials?	◯	◯	◯

6 Pitfalls checklist
Things to check before making your project

	Project 1	Project 2	Project 3
Can your work project be assembled? Work out an order of assembly	◯	◯	◯
Are you trying to use materials which will be difficult or impossible to obtain?	◯	◯	◯
Can you use cheaper materials to do the job just as well?	◯	◯	◯
Does the working drawing show everything you intend?	◯	◯	◯
Are all the processes you propose possible? Are any going to be difficult to achieve?	◯	◯	◯
Have you planned the manufacture in a logical sequence?	◯	◯	◯
Will you be able to get your project out of workshop/home/upstairs?	◯	◯	◯
Do you have the skills to make what you are proposing?	◯	◯	◯
Will you have difficulty getting any of the materials/components which you need?	◯	◯	◯

7 Working drawing checklist

	Project 1	Project 2	Project 3

Someone else should be able to make your design from your working drawing. Can they?

Have all dimensions been included?

Are all details of materials shown?

Is it clear how the parts are joined together?

Have you included a list of parts or a cutting list?

This viewed from front → FRONT elevation

This viewed from end → END elevation

This viewed from above → PLAN

Cutting list

Name   Project title   Scale

8 Planning checklist
Use this to either plan your whole project or the manufacture

	Project 1	Project 2	Project 3
Are you writing a planning schedule, slip chart or project diary?	◯	◯	◯
Have you listed the tasks in a logical order?	◯	◯	◯
Have you taken advice on how long each task will take?	◯	◯	◯
Are you thinking ahead?	◯	◯	◯
Does your planning show possible alternative tasks?	◯	◯	◯
Does your planning help you avoid wasting time?	◯	◯	◯
Are you keeping a record of what you do?	◯	◯	◯
Will you order/obtain materials in advance of needing them?	◯	◯	◯
Have you planned to make best use of your lesson time/homework/holidays?	◯	◯	◯

9 Assessment checklist
Things to check whilst making your project

	Project 1	Project 2	Project 3
Am I using suitable materials and manufacturing techniques?	◯	◯	◯
Am I working accurately to the working drawing and do all parts fit each other?	◯	◯	◯
Have I taken trouble with the finish?	◯	◯	◯
Does my project work properly?	◯	◯	◯
Am I working safely, obeying all the workshop safety rules and wearing safety clothing?	◯	◯	◯
Am I working to schedule?	◯	◯	◯

10 Evaluation checklist

Answer the following questions honestly. Make clear drawings where it helps the explanation

	Project 1	Project 2	Project 3
Does your finished product look like what you intended it to? If no, what's different and why?	◯	◯	◯
Does your finished project do what it was meant to? If yes, how well? If no, why not?	◯	◯	◯
What problems did you have in making your project?	◯	◯	◯
If you remade your project, how could you **plan** your **time** better?	◯	◯	◯
What are the satisfactory **and** unsatisfactory features of your design?	◯	◯	◯
What changes would you make to overcome the unsatisfactory features of your design?	◯	◯	◯
If you were to repeat this project what changes would you make? Why would you make them?	◯	◯	◯

11 Folio checklist
Things to check before handing in your folio

	Project 1	Project 2	Project 3

Make sure that the folio for each project has:

	Project 1	Project 2	Project 3
A cover with name, project title and candidate number (if you know it)	◯	◯	◯
An index or contents page	◯	◯	◯
All pages numbered neatly	◯	◯	◯
A heading for each section: 'Need', 'Research', 'Ideas', etc	◯	◯	◯
All pages held together securely	◯	◯	◯

Glossary of terms

A

Acrylic A plastics material, commercially known as 'Perspex'. Sometimes referred to as PMMA

Acid rain Industrial waste such as sulphur dioxide is absorbed into the atmosphere which then falls in the rain damaging the countryside and buildings

Adhesives Another word for glues. Used to bond materials together

Alloying Fusing together a metal usually with another metal or metals to produce a material with different properties

Ampere Unit of electrical current often abbreviated AMP

Analysis To break down into smaller parts. Often associated with the early stages of the design process

Annealing To soften a material such as steel, copper or aluminium by heating and then allowing to cool

Anodizing Producing a surface of film oxide on aluminium by an electrolytic process

Anthropometrics Literally the measurements of man. Essential when designing things for people

B

BDMS Bright drawn mild steel

Bearings Designed to reduce friction between moving parts

Brainstorming A method of developing ideas. Everyone suggests his or her ideas which are then written down. Sometimes silly ideas are suggested but these occasionally develop into good solutions

Brief A set of instructions on what you have to do or what you are intending to design

BSI British Standards Institution. Responsible for codes of practice, such as drawing standards PP 7308

C

CAD Computer-aided design

CAM Computer-aided manufacturing

Case hardening Mild steel can have its surface hardened by 'soaking' red hot steel in a carbon rich powder. It is reheated and then quenched in cold water

Ceramic Made from clay and fused at high temperature in a kiln

CFC Chloroflurocarbon: associated with aerosols and a contributor to the breaking down of the ozone layer

CNC Computer numerical control

Coursework That part of your CDT course, consisting of design and make projects, which is marked by your teacher and moderated by an external examiner or assessor

Counterbalance Usually a weight used to compensate for the weight of some load, e.g. a crane is prevented from toppling over by the use of a heavy weight which compensates for the load

Component An individual part of which many may combine to make a complete object

Concrete Sand, gravel and cement mixed dry and then water added. A chemical reaction causes it to set hard. Very good compression strength

Conservation To save from destruction. Organizations such as Greenpeace ensure that we never forget how important this is

Construction An arrangement of parts or components

Corrosion Usually associated with the 'rotting' of metals due to the action of the air

D

Degassing Removing trapped gas from molten metal immediately before it is poured into a mould

Design Is an activity which uses a wide range of experiences, knowledge and skills to find the best solution to a problem, within certain constraints. It is far more than just problem solving. It involves the whole process of producing a solution from conception to production

Design Council Formed in 1972, it offers an advisory and information service to designers and manufacturers. Products judged to be of 'good' design are displayed in the Council's centres in London, Cardiff, Glasgow and Belfast

Draft When making a pattern for sand casting or vacuum forming it is essential that there is a taper or 'draft' so that the pattern can be removed

Ductile A material which can be stretched without easily breaking

Dynamic force A moving force

E

Efficiency Working with the minimum of lost effort. Machines can be made efficient by use of smooth bearings and lubrication

Ergonomics The study of finding ways to help humans work more efficiently

Evaluation Making judgments about the suitability of your design and the way you go about producing it. Such judgments can be made during the design stages and at the conclusion of the project

Exploded views Three-dimensional drawings where the individual components are shown separately

Examination group Two or more of the older GCE or CSE

examination boards combined together to administer GCSE examinations. There are six such groups

F

Face marks Accurate and true surfaces from which measurements are taken and marked with face side and face edge marks

Fibonacci series A series of numbers where each number is found by adding the two previous ones, e.g. 1,1,2,3,5,8,13,21 etc

Fibreglass The common term used for GRP (glass reinforced polyester)

Finish The treatment of the surface of a material

Former A shaped block around which (acrylic, for example) is bent or formed

Friends of the Earth An organization concerned with issues such as acid rain, dumping of poisoned waste, etc

Function What you expect your design solution to do. The function may be practical or aesthetic

Fuse An electrical item which blows to protect an electrical circuit when it becomes overloaded

G

Generic A name meaning members of the same group or family, e.g. metal is the generic name for steel, copper, aluminium

Golden mean Proportions based upon successive numbers in the Fibonacci series. Such proportions are generally regarded as 'attractive', e.g. a rectangle of 5 × 8 or 13 × 21

H

Hardening and tempering The process of heating carbon steel to red heat and cooling quickly in oil is called hardening. Brittleness is removed by further gentle heating and cooling in water

I

Injection moulding Injecting a molten material under pressure into a mould (known as a die)

Isometric A method of drawing in three dimensions. Horizontal lines are drawn at 30° to the horizontal and vertical lines remain vertical

J

Joule The unit in which energy is measured

Joining The fastening of two or more parts together

K

Kilo One thousand. Used in front of others words, e.g. one kilometre = one thousand metres

L

Laminating Making something by building up thin layers such as GRP or 'bent' timber, as in some school furniture

LEAG London East Anglian Group

Logo (logogram) A symbol used to identify a person, company or organization

M

Malleable The ability to be easily distorted under pressure without breaking. Malleability often improves with heating

Market research Investigating needs and requirements often by means of a questionnaire

Marketing The process by which a product is 'sold' to the public. It includes such things as market research and advertising

MEG Midland Examining Group

Mitre An angle of 45°. Picture frames commonly have their corners mitred

Multimeter Used to test electrical circuits. It can usually measure voltage, current, and resistance

N

National Criteria A set of rules laid down for all GCSE subjects

NEA Northern Examining Association

NISEC Northern Ireland Schools Examinations Council

O

Oblique At an angle. Oblique projection is a form of drawing where the front view is drawn parallel to the vertical plane and the top and sides are drawn at 45° to the horizontal plane

Orthographic projection A type of drawing, consisting of often three views, drawn to scale, each taken at 90° to each other

Oxidization The surface of most metals will combine with the atmosphere to oxidize, e.g. rusting of ferrous metals. Oxides on metal can make soldering and brazing difficult

Ozone layer A condensed form of oxygen (O_3) which forms a layer above the surface of the earth protecting us from harmful ultra-violet rays

P

PAR Planed all round

Perspective The appearance that objects which are further away look smaller

Plastic memory The ability of some materials to return to their original moulded shape after reheating

Polymer Long chain molecules. The main characteristic of plastics

Potential difference Often referred to as voltage. The pressure which 'pushes' electricity around a circuit

Preservative Material with which other materials are treated to prevent them from reacting to the atmosphere, e.g. creosote

Primary research Original research that is done by you, such as discussion, interview, survey or experiment

Proportion The relationship of one part to another. Sizes are often said to be *in proportion* when they appeal to one's visual sense of balance

Project A design task usually in the form of a design and make activity beginning with a need

Prototype A trial version of a product

R

Research The gathering of information to assist in the production of a solution to a need

Resistance The ability to prevent the flow of electrical current

S

Scale Drawing to scale means drawing so that all parts are in the same proportion, i.e. if the width is one half real size then other dimensions are one half real size also

Seasoning Careful drying of 'green' timber to make it usable in, say, furniture

Secondary research Research done by other people, e.g. in books, magazines, etc

SEG Southern Examining Group

Shake A natural split in timber often caused by fast seasoning

Silver solder Solder which melts at a higher temperature than soft (tin/lead) solder. It is an alloy of silver, copper, zinc and cadmium

Silver steel Precision ground carbon steel. It does **not** contain any silver

Soft solder A group of low temperature solders made from tin and lead

Solenoid A device whereby an iron core is pulled into a coil of wire when an electrical current flows in the coil

Solution Your way of satisfying a need or providing an answer to a problem

Specification A list of targets

Structure An arrangement of parts designed to withstand a load

Stable Not easily moved, changed or destroyed

Swarf The waste material associated, usually, with drilling, milling and turning on the lathe

System A set of connected things or parts, organized to perform a function or functions

Synthesis Bringing together the various parts of a project

T

Technology is the application of man's knowledge and understanding to satisfy the needs of society

Thermoforming Material which becomes soft at higher temperature can then be shaped e.g. vacuum forming

Toggle mechanism A mechanism often used in holding devices such as mole wrenches and the clamps on vacuum forming machines. It has a quick locking and release action. An umbrella is locked in position by a toggle mechanism

V

Vacuum forming A process whereby a softened (by heat) thermoplastic material is formed over a shaped former by the application of a vacuum

W

Weld Joining components by allowing the parts to become 'melted' together. This can be achieved by heating or in the case of some plastics by the use of chemicals

WJEC Welsh Joint Education Committee

Index